TAKE THE STAIRS!

A Discussion of Character, its Development and its Continuous Improvement

Terry Drabant

DEDICATION

This book is dedicated to the US Air Force Academy and to the more than 38,000 men and women graduates of USAFA, beginning with the first class in 1959, who make up the "Long Blue Line".

This book is also dedicated to Brigadier General Mal Wakin who taught Philosophy at USAFA from 1959 until his retirement in 1996. Since then he has continued to lecture every cadet class on philosophy and character. In 1964, I attended then-Captain Wakin's Philosophy 310 class at USAFA, where I was introduced to philosophy, and where my eyes were finally and completely opened to the importance of the development of my character and its continuous improvement.

ACKNOWLEDGEMENTS

I have received encouragement, support, ideas, and corrections from many people during the time that I have worked on this book. First I would like to thank my wife, friend and soul mate, Toni, and the three adults who will always be our kids, Robin, Karen and Michael.

I would also like to thank (in alphabetical order) Air Force Colonel (retired) Tom Berry (USAFA class of 71), Air Force Brigadier General Dana Born (USAFA class of 83), Marine Lieutenant Colonel Tim Born (USNA class of 75), Audra Craig, Ron Craig (USAFA class of 91), Angela Heise, Bart Holaday (USAFA Class of 65), Neil King, Air Force Lieutenant Austen Lefevbre (USAFA class of 04), Dorota Mroczek, Stefan Mroczek, Jon Rambeau, Cheryl Songster, Tim Songster (USAFA class of 93), Ken Stoltman USAFA class of 94, Air Force Lieutenant Brian Sump (USAFA class of 06), Deon Viergutz, Bill Wecker (USAFA class of 63), and especially, Air Force Brigadier General (retired) Mal Wakin.

TABLE OF CONTENTS

BEGINNING

The date was June 26th, 1961, and I was 18 years old and had just arrived at the US Air Force Academy (USAFA) as a new Basic Cadet. I was one of 822 Basic Cadets in the class that would graduate in 1965. I was very nervous, but I thought that I was ready for the extremely tough first year as a Doolie. This is the nickname for freshman at USAFA, which is derived from the

Greek word "duolos" meaning slave. In hindsight, I had no idea how physically, mentally and emotionally challenging the next four years would be.

I will never forget that first day. I had flown to Colorado earlier that day from Chicago (300 feet above sea level). USAFA is located just north of Colorado Springs in the foothills of the Rampart Range in the Rocky Mountains at 7250 feet above sea level. As we arrived at USAFA, we were met by members of the senior class. They would be our instructors and our military superiors for the next eight weeks of Basic Cadet Summer. We were immediately put through a session of individual instruction on military drill. This was done incrementally as we were directed to run from one upperclass Cadet to another and report in. We would be at attention, standing, marching, running in place or running between upperclassmen all during this process.

Instruction consisted of constant "in your face" yelling, rapid commands, correction of our many mistakes, and twenty push-ups each time we made a mistake. We learned how to stand at attention with our shoulders back and chin in, how to march, how to report as we were told to run to the next Cadet ("Sir, Basic Cadet Drabant reporting as ordered."). We were taught our three basic answers to any question from a superior—"Yes, sir", "No sir", and "No excuse, sir."

We also quickly learned that failure to answer a question correctly or failure to act with excellence and enthusiasm (including the push-ups) resulted in additional correction. This was very similar to the treatment that Richard Gere received from Lou Gossett Jr. in the movie, An Officer and a Gentleman. The only difference was that it seemed as if we each had our own personal set of multiple drill instructors, and each one was able to dedicate full time to our poor performance.

After about an hour of drill instruction (it seemed as if it was all day), we were then marched at attention to the barbershop for a two-minute haircut. We were even required to sit at attention during this haircut. This was a buzz cut that would be the required haircut for the next eight weeks. After our haircuts, we were marched and formed up in our assigned summer squadrons on the Terrazzo (at USAFA, it is pronounced te-rät'-so). This is a large marching and formation area in the center of the Cadet area bordered by the academic building in the east (Fairchild Hall), the original dormitory in the north (Vandenberg Hall), the dining hall (Mitchell Hall) and a second dormitory in the south (Sijan Hall, completed in 1969 and dedicated in 1976), and the Chapel, administration building (Harmon Hall) and the student center (Arnold Hall) on the west.

The Cadet area is cut into the side of a hill so that Vandenberg, Fairchild, Mitchell and Sijan Halls have floors that are below the level of the Terrazzo. The gymnasium and athletic fields are north of Vandenberg Hall in the valley, and are much further below the Terrazzo and below the first floor of Vandenberg Hall.

While waiting on the Terrazzo for the rest of our class to finish their haircuts, the yelling, instruction, correction and push-ups continued, all the while trying to improve our ragtag performance. I have no idea how many push-ups I did the first day. I certainly did a lot more than I ever thought that I could do, but not enough to keep the upperclass Cadets happy. Once we were all formed up, we were brought to attention and sworn in by reciting an oath of allegiance to the United States.

I, _____, having been appointed a Cadet, in the United States Air Force, do solemnly swear (or affirm) that I will support and defend the Constitution of the United States against all enemies, foreign and domestic, that I will bear true faith and allegiance to the same; that I take this obligation freely, without any mental reservation or purpose of evasion, and that I will well and faithfully discharge the duties of the office upon which I am about to enter. SO HELP ME GOD.

We were now officially members of the US Air Force.

After the swearing-in ceremony, we were marched to our dorm rooms. We were kept at attention and marched from one of the fourth floor entrances of Vandenberg Hall up to the sixth floor where the room that I would share with one other Doolie was located. Initially, our dorm rooms were the only place that we were allowed to stand or sit at ease as long as there was no upperclassman in the room. This would later be expanded to include classrooms and the academic area. Shortly after we were placed in our assigned rooms, we were marched at attention in small groups by our element leader to be measured and to collect our initial set of uniforms. We marched down to the first floor of Vandenberg Hall where we were issued two duffle bags full of uniforms—everything from our skivvies out.

We were then led to one of the first floor stairwells and told to run with our two duffle bags up six flights of stairs. I looked longingly at the elevator, but our element leader chewed me out for "gazing" while at attention, ordered 20 push-ups, and said, while leading the way, "We take the stairs." As you can imagine, running up six flights of stairs, carrying two duffle bags, at 7250 feet above sea level is quite a physical and aerobic challenge! Little did I know that, in that one statement, I had been introduced to a fundamental truth that would be critical to me throughout my life. With appreciation to Sophocles, who said over 2400 years ago, "Success is dependent upon effort." **This book is about the importance of taking the stairs in both our personal and professional lives.**

CHAPTER 1

CHALLENGE and SELF-ASSESSMENT

As I stood in the bottom of the stairwell on the first floor of Vandenberg Hall that first day as a Basic Cadet, in theory, I had three choices—I could refuse to go up the stairs, I could try to take the elevator, or I could take the stairs. In practice, if I wanted to stay at the Air Force Academy and in the Air Force, I had only one very painfully obvious choice—that was to do as I was told and to take the stairs. The consequences of not taking the stairs would have been both very real and very immediate. Of course I took the stairs.

Over the next year, the next four years, and throughout my life I would be faced again and again with these same three choices—take the stairs, take the elevator or stay on the same floor. Although, as time progressed, the penalties for not taking the stairs became both less obvious and less immediate.

Also, during that first day of Basic Cadet Summer it was made very apparent to me that I would be required to demonstrate enthusiasm, maximum effort and excellence if I wanted to survive. Merely surviving by "meeting minimum requirements" that first year would not be possible. Failure to demonstrate enthusiasm, maximum effort and excellence was the USAFA equivalent of bleeding in the water to sharks. This would cause a Doolie to be identified as an attitude problem and would result in "special attention" (in later years called "special instruction") from the upperclassmen.

"Special attention" could best be described as a ½ hour or longer one-on-one session with one or more upperclassmen who acted as if they were aerobics instructors from Hell. These sessions would occur during very valuable Doolie time when the rest of our classmates would otherwise be in their rooms studying or preparing for inspections. A session would consist of more "in your face" yelling during difficult exercises (usually with a rifle), being driven to excel up to, and through failure, followed by additional training and correction.

One of the outcomes of this process was that the upperclassmen proved to us that we could do much, much more than we thought that we were capable of accomplishing.

After one of these sessions, I would return to my room with every muscle quivering from the effort, and I would be both physically and emotionally exhausted. We Doolies learned very quickly that these "special attention" sessions were to be avoided if at all possible. We could reduce the frequency of occurrence by enthusiastically executing every command correctly with maximum excellence, but these sessions would not be completely avoidable. Every Doolie would experience many "special attention" sessions over their first year.

In high school I had decided that I wanted to become a member of the Air Force, and to serve the nation through military service as a pilot. I wanted to accomplish that objective by attending USAFA.

On the first day of Basic Cadet Summer my "goal horizon" quickly became shorter and shorter. During that first hour of the first day of drill instruction, I was worrying about surviving the first year. After we took our duffle bags up the six flights of stairs and to our rooms, I was worried about surviving the eight weeks of Basic Cadet Summer. By the end of the first day, my goal was to survive a day at a time. During some of the longer training runs, running the obstacle course and some of the "special attention" sessions, it was to survive a step at a time. To paraphrase the ancient Chinese proverb from Lao-Tzu, my personal journey of a thousand miles began at the bottom of a stairwell in Vandenberg Hall with but a single step—up the stairs.

Entering USAFA is a lot like being at the top of the stairwell before you arrive and then finding yourself at the bottom of the stairwell both literally and physically on your first day. As with all top-notch universities, the extremely selective entrance criteria for USAFA results in an entry class of very successful high school graduates.

Once you enter, not only do you find yourself pushed all the way to (and through) failure as a Doolie, but you also find that it seems that all of your classmates must be over-achieving valedictorian jocks. Each new Doolie undergoes this severe shock as they instantly transition upon arrival from very successful high school graduate to a "failing Doolie", and then they undergo a further shock when they start to compare themselves to their classmates, as they don't necessarily see all of their classmates' failures.

With all of the different demands placed on the Doolies, it is hard not to come to the conclusion that each of us was continuing to fail at some part of our responsibilities, and that each of us were, at best, average when compared to our classmates. More than once, I questioned my career goals and the path that I had selected to accomplish those goals.

For me, the good news was that I had decided upon a demanding set of career goals and a very demanding preparatory path very early in my career. The bad news was that I was also finding out very early in my career how difficult it would be to accomplish those goals.

Each of our lives consists of constant decisions/choices. The first and most important decisions that we make are our goals. Yogi Berra said it best when he said, "You got to be careful if you don't know where you're going, because you might not get there." A goal without a plan (the stairs) is not a goal—it is a wish, and it is a wish that will not be fulfilled. No decision about goals and/or no plan is, in fact, a decision to do nothing (stay at the bottom of the stairwell). The longer the decision is delayed, the longer that each of will stay at the bottom of the stairwell.

Over the next four years at USAFA I was forced to "take the stairs" in multiple ways. The first and most obvious "take the stairs" requirement was the military discipline. The second "take the stairs" requirement was a rigorous Bachelor of Science academic curriculum where graduation was required in four years with five or six classes a semester. The third "take the stairs" requirement was to complete the physical discipline of Basic Cadet Summer, take special physical fitness courses such as survival swimming, boxing and unarmed combat, and prepare for and pass a physical fitness test (including the obstacle course) every year. The fourth "take the stairs" requirement was to participate in either intercollegiate or intramural sports every semester. What quickly became very clear to me was that if I wanted to graduate from the Air Force Academy, I would have to take all of the prescribed "stairs", in addition to all of the stairs in Vandenberg and Fairchild Halls.

After completing my Doolie (fourth class) year, I thought that I could relax a little more. At some point in my sophomore (third class) year, I realized that I wanted more than to just finish the experience at USAFA. Merely finishing the experience would be to fall back to a "meets minimum requirements" status. I had to re-learn that if I did not maintain my excellence and enthusiasm, that I would not be successful.

These lessons were not as obvious and nor was the feedback as immediate as it was when I was a Doolie. One academic example that occurs at every college and is also true at USAFA is prerequisite courses. I learned very quickly that it was not sufficient to merely get a good grade. I had to actually learn the material, as that knowledge would be both assumed and required in the next class, and the next class would be more difficult. This, of course, is such an obvious concept, but unfortunately I needed to experience this myself once or twice it in order to learn it.

Also, as an upperclassman, by definition I was going to be an example for the new Doolies. Was I going to be a positive or a negative example? How could I expect excellence and enthusiasm from the Doolies if I did not model that excellence and enthusiasm myself? Again this lesson was not as obvious or as immediately learned as it was when I was a Doolie. When I first became an upperclassman (sophomore), there were many opportunities to "take the elevator", but if I was going to set an example as a leader of the new Doolies, as my first element leader had done before me that first day, my position as a leader would require me to enthusiastically lead the way up the stairs.

That desire for enthusiastic excellence and to set an example as a leader required that I "take the stairs" at every opportunity. Looking back on my four years at USAFA, I had inadvertently discovered the **First Principle of Taking the Stairs—Challenge: We should challenge ourselves by aiming high and selecting challenging and laudable life goals, and then when our life goals require taking the stairs, we should take the stairs immediately with enthusiasm and excellence.**

In my junior and senior years at USAFA, my choices would be even less obvious than they had been my first two years. Ironically, one of my lessons came from the Vandenberg Hall elevators. First- and second-classmen (seniors and juniors) were allowed to use the elevators in Vandenberg Hall, but even those elevators seemed perversely designed to re-enforce the principle of taking the stairs. Because the elevators are so very slow and are frequently dedicated to hauling maintenance supplies, and because of the time demands placed on Cadets, it is faster and more reliable to take the stairs. By waiting for the elevator, there would be a good chance that the user would be late for the next class or formation. I made the mistake of doing this once. After that, I took the stairs.

During my junior and senior years, as I was assigned to leadership positions at USAFA, I discovered that I was not always effective as a leader. Also, academic classes began to require much more analytical and creative effort. I was not always as effective in a class as I needed to be. Another of the lessons of Doolie year had come back to me. As a Doolie, "No excuse, sir" is the only answer to a why question about your failure to perform with excellence and enthusiasm.

This "no-excuses" mentality became a critical ingredient to my process of introspection and self-improvement. If I thought of myself as a victim or blamed others for my lack of performance, or thought that my performance was good enough, I would continue to perform at the same level and make no improvements. Benjamin Franklin said, "Insanity is doing the same thing over and over and expecting different results."

I had inadvertently learned that in order to be successful, I would have to continue to say "No excuse, sir" to myself, to learn to self-assess my current actions, results and skills, to figure out how to improve those, and to look for additional skills and experiences that would be valuable to me in my future career. I would have to plan ahead and look for these opportunities.

The discipline that was imposed upon me as a Doolie would now have to become self-discipline. It took me a little longer, but I had also stumbled upon the **Second Principle of Taking the Stairs—Self-Assessment: We should frequently and critically assess our performance and challenge ourselves to find additional stairs to climb and even some stairs that we should re-climb with enthusiasm and excellence.**

A major milestone for Cadets occurs in May at the end of second-class (junior) year. This is when the annual ring dance is held, and the Cadets receive their USAFA class rings. I was a member of the ring committee that helped design the ring. Each class selects a class motto and a falcon design that is put on the class side of the ring. Appropriately to this chapter, the class of 65 selected the motto "Provocationem Accipimus", which is Latin for "We accept the challenge."

Frequently we see news stories about people who are very successful, and the story would sometimes imply that this was an overnight success based only on ability or luck or both. The more that you delve into the background and experiences of these individuals, the more you find that the success was not an overnight event, but rather, it was a both a journey and a process that was based on three factors.

The first factor that differentiates successful individuals is that they defined for themselves a set of very challenging and laudable goals ("aim high"). Henry David Thoreau said it best when he wrote, "In the long run, you hit only what you aim at: Therefore aim high."

The second factor is that they demonstrate a significant amount of continuous hard work ("take the stairs"). President Thomas Jefferson said, "I'm a great believer in luck, and I find the harder I work the more I have of it."

The third factor is that they exhibit both self-discipline and a willingness to self-assess and self-correct ("re-climb stairs"). Anthony J. D'Angelo said, "Become addicted to constant and never-ending self-improvement."

No decision about goals is a decision to do nothing ("stay at the bottom of the stairwell"). Why can't our decision be to make no decision? Why can't our goals be to have no goals? Why can't we just "go with the flow"? These seem to be the questions of many individuals today. How much does society owe us? To what are we entitled? Forty-five years ago, President John F. Kennedy said, "Ask not what your country can do for you. Ask what you can do for your country." In life, we are entitled to only what we earn, and we are respected for only what we have accomplished. This demands that we start with goals.

To achieve challenging and laudable goals, there is generally an apparent hard path ("take the stairs") an apparent easy path ("take the elevator") and a do nothing path ("stay at the bottom of the stairwell"). The apparent hard path will consist of incremental goals ("each floor") that are required in order to achieve our final goals. In my experience, I have never observed a shortcut elevator to success. I have, however, observed apparent elevator opportunities that appear to avoid a specific set of stairs.

Like the elevators in Vandenberg Hall, you can push the button and then wait forever, or conversely, when the elevator finally arrives, it doesn't take you to where you want to go. Usually, individuals who look for and/or take these elevator opportunities end up staying where they are and/or end up lacking a specific skill or experience that is essential to their continued success. This lack usually results in their ultimate failure.

All of the successful people whom I know very well or have observed over the years were successful because they have worked extremely hard all their lives. The comparisons between the two golfers, Tiger Woods and John Daly, are striking. Very early in their careers, each was touted as a naturally gifted athlete who would likely become one of the best golfers in the PGA. The differences in accomplishments between the two are night and day due to Tiger's discipline, his training regimen, and his willingness to self-assess and make corrections in order to improve. His decision in 2003 to completely re-do his swing when the golf pundits said that he was at the top of his game, indicates his self-correcting drive for excellence. Tiger Woods said, "[Why would I] change my swing after I won the Masters by 12 shots? Well, I thought I could become better."

We can't all be Tiger Woods, but as Richard Bach said, "Argue for your limitations and, sure enough, they're yours." For each of us, maximum effort, self-discipline, continuous self-assessment and self-correction will be much more critical to our success than will any self-perceived limitations of our ability.

Vince Lombardi said, "The price of success is hard work, dedication to the job at hand, and the determination that whether we win or lose, we have applied the best of ourselves to the task at hand."

Each of us must aim high, take the stairs, self-assess and self-correct in order to accomplish our life goals.

CHAPTER 2

PREPARATION, PERSEVERENCE and CONSTANCY

After four tough years, graduation day finally arrived on the 9th of June 1965. I was proud to graduate with a Bachelor of Science degree in Engineering as one of the 517 graduates of the class of 1965. However, I was one of eight graduates in my class who would not be serving in the military. My specific case was due to a serious back injury incurred while competing in Judo. Instead, my future was destined to be in the engineering/business world.

Graduation day was for me, simultaneously, one of the happiest and one of the saddest days of my life. I had just completed a very tough four years and would be an Air Force Academy Graduate, but this was to be the last day that I would wear an Air Force uniform. This was very traumatic for me, because of my desire to serve and to be a pilot. Although I had "failed" and a military career was closed to me, the good news was that, as a USAFA graduate, I was both well prepared and in high demand for entry level engineering positions.

Looking back, it is now obvious to me that everyone goes through this process of career opportunity doors being closed. The period between the ages of 13 and 25 is perhaps the most defining and, frequently, the most traumatic period of life for each of us. At age 13, every future career is possible—from astronaut to zoologist and every letter in between. By age 25, doors have been incrementally closed as a result of classes taken in high school, high school performance, university acceptance, university degree, academic major selection and performance, and, for some, advanced degree program acceptance, degree selection and performance.

It is also extremely important to make the decisions that keep the most career opportunity doors open. These are usually the most difficult courses. As an example, failure to take math every year through calculus in high school closes a large number of career doors. I also found this to be a very important concept later in my business career. Like the chess player who can only see a certain number of moves into the future, the real question is which move seems to put us in the best position for future moves?

The same door-closing process occurs in the sports world. Many sports require both starting at an early age and a serious focus in order to be competitive in high school, college and beyond. I think that this is also a case of preparation for any serious endeavor. The Boy Scout motto, "Be Prepared", originated by founder Lord Robert Baden-Powell, is very relevant to academics, sports, and careers in both the military and civilian world and to life in general.

The more "full spectrum" preparedness that we can obtain before climbing the next required set of stairs, the better our performance will be, and the more satisfaction that we will feel. Author J. B. Matthews said, "Unless a man has trained himself for his chance, the chance will only make him look ridiculous." The best way to avoid being surprised, and to avoid it suddenly becoming "too hard" is to take the initiative to make it hard on ourselves now! Henry Ford said, "Before everything else, getting ready is the secret to success."

These observations have led me to the **Third Principle of Taking the Stairs—Preparation: We should start early and take the more difficult stairs. These will have the most doors at the top and the most life options. The better our performance on the stairs, the more we control our own destiny and the higher we will climb.**

Looking back, I did not take all of the stairs or start early all of the time. We can't change the past, but each of us can change the future by starting today to take the more difficult stairs to prepare for our life goals.

The downside of pursuing any very difficult path is the risk of not successfully completing that path. The USAFA class of 1965 had started with 822 members in June of 1961, and 517 graduated in June of 1965. That is an attrition rate of 38%. However, I believe that each and every starting member of our class gained significantly from the USAFA experience. President Theodore Roosevelt said, "It is not the critic who counts, not the man who points out how the strong man stumbled, or where the doer of deeds could have done better. The credit belongs to the man who is actually in the arena, whose face is marred by dust and sweat and blood, who strives valiantly, who errs and comes short again and again, who knows the great enthusiasms, the great devotions, and spends himself in a worthy cause, who at best knows achievement and who at the worst if he fails at least fails while daring greatly so that his place shall never be with those cold and timid souls who know neither victory nor defeat." I know of numerous classmates who did not graduate but went on to complete their degrees at other top-notch universities and had very successful careers as Air Force officers through ROTC, company presidents, doctors, lawyers or entrepreneurs.

After completing their degree (at USAFA or some place else) each member of the class of 1965 was now at the bottom of a new stairwell, either as a Second Lieutenant starting pilot training or as graduate school student, or as a "newbie" starting their first assignment. For those of us not commissioned, we either entered graduate school or started as an entry-level professional in a new career.

Looking back at my USAFA experience, there was another lesson that I had learned. This was, for me, the most important lesson. This was the **Fourth Principle of Taking the Stairs—Perseverance: We must persevere when the stairs get hard, and, if the stairs are blocked, then find a way around the block. If there is no way around the blockage, then we must pick ourselves up and find another set of challenging stairs to climb.**

So, in July of 1965, after major back surgery, I again started at the bottom of the stairwell. This time it was in the engineering/business world. John Wooden said, "Don't let what you cannot do interfere with what you can do." So I dedicated myself to be successful on the new set of stairs.

This "bottom of the stairwell" process was to repeat itself over and over during my career as I reached each new level of experience, was promoted or started each new assignment. I would be required to prove myself over and over. It was not a straight line to career success, and these first four principles would occasionally require reinforcement. There would be times when my performance was not good enough—just like Doolie year. "Experience is what you get when you don't get what you want." is an appropriate quote attributed to writer, Dan Stanford. But this quote is only true if we are willing to say "No excuse, sir" and learn from the experience.

Over the years, I grew from programmer/systems analyst to manager to project manager to business area director to vice-president to division president. When I retired after almost 40 years, I was a corporate officer of the Lockheed Martin Corporation. The first four principles of taking the stairs had been, and continue to be critical to my success.

I looked for the most challenging assignments, and I looked for assignments that would provide me with the most experience. This left the most career doors open. I looked for continuous challenge, and this honed my skills. I deliberately forced myself to the "bottom of the stairs" for experience. I never let myself get too comfortable. Most importantly to my success I continued to "take those stairs."

Along the way I observed others who concluded that they had "arrived" at some destination, and then relaxed and stopped "taking the stairs." The result I noticed was that not only did they go no further in their career, but, in fact, the effort to get them to that specific destination ("floor") was also required to keep them there. Once they stopped "taking the stairs", their career success quickly declined.

George Sheehan said, "Excellence is not something attained & put in a trophy case. It is not sought after, achieved, and, thereafter, a steady state. It is a momentary phenomenon, a rare conjunction of body, mind & spirit at one's peak. Should I come to that peak, I cannot stay there. Like Sisyphus, I must start each day at the bottom and work back up to the top. And then beyond that peak to another and yet another."

These observations and experiences became the **Fifth Principle of Taking the Stairs—Constancy. We can't ever stop climbing the stairs. We must persevere through our whole life. Once we stop climbing the stairs, they become a**

slow escalator going down, and other climbers will rapidly pass us.

This requirement to continually "take the stairs" is true, even at the top of the corporate pyramid. As you read about the successful CEO's of major companies, you will frequently read that they are working as hard as they ever did during their career. The continued success of their companies cannot be taken for granted, and they must continue to work very hard to assure that success. That hard work and their continued success are what allow them to continue as CEO. Of course, not everyone will make it to the top of the corporate pyramid and not everyone wants to go that far.

Whatever our career and life aspirations, it will take significant effort to accomplish them, and it will require continued significant effort to maintain them. Stephen King said, "Talent is cheaper than table salt. What separates the talented individual from the successful one is a lot of hard work." Failure to recognize this and/or failure to execute will result in not achieving and sustaining our goals.

In summary, in order to achieve career and life success, there are five critical principles of taking the stairs. Each builds on the previous, and all are necessary to assure our career success. The five principles of taking the stairs are:

1. <u>**Challenge:**</u> **We should challenge ourselves by aiming high and selecting challenging and laudable life goals, and then, when our life goals require taking the stairs, we should take the stairs immediately with enthusiasm and excellence.** Robert H. Schuller said, "Goals are not only absolutely necessary to motivate us. They are essential to really keep us alive."

2. **Self-Assessment: We should frequently and critically assess our performance and challenge ourselves to find additional stairs to climb and even some stairs that we should re-climb with enthusiasm and excellence.** Marie du Deffand said, "Let us strive to improve ourselves, for we cannot remain stationary; one either progresses or retrogrades."

3. **Preparation: We should start early and take the more difficult stairs. These will have the most doors at the top and the most life options. The better our performance on the stairs, the more we control our own destiny and the higher we will climb.** "Bear" Bryant said, "It's not the will to win, but the will to prepare to win that makes the difference."

4. **Perseverance: We must persevere when the stairs get hard, and, if the stairs are blocked, then find a way around the block. If there is no way around the blockage, then we must pick ourselves up and find another set of challenging stairs to climb.** Michael Jordan said, "If you run into a wall, don't turn around and give up. Figure out how to climb it, go through it, or work your way around it."

5. **Constancy. We can't ever stop climbing the stairs. We must persevere through our whole life. Once we stop climbing the stairs, they become a slow escalator going down, and other climbers will rapidly pass us.** Ralph Waldo Emerson said, "All great masters are chiefly distinguished by the power of adding a second, a third, and perhaps a fourth step in a continuous line. Many a man has

taken the first step. With every additional step you enhance immensely the value of your first."

All five of these principles are necessary for career and life success, but they are not the only requirements. And you thought this book would be an easy read! This is a "take the stairs" book. In real life, we are constantly faced with multiple sets of stairs from which to choose (or to do nothing).

In point of fact, before we take the stairs we cannot see what is on the next landing. And some of the stairs go no further than the next landing. Some stairs go to a landing with only one set of stairs visible, while other stairs go to a landing with multiple sets of stairs going further up. Some stairs will take us to a landing that is lower than our current position. The stairs that we experience in the real world seem to have been drawn by artist M. C. Escher. His lithographs entitled *Relativity* (1953) and *Ascending and Descending* (1960) come to mind. You can find these on the web site at www.mcescher.com in the Galleries link.

How do we know which set of stairs to take? If we look closely, there are indicators at the bottom of each set of stairs. I directly defined only two of those indicators in the first two chapters, but I alluded to two others. The two indicators that should stand out from reading this far are based on **challenge** and **perseverance**. Simply said, **we should pick the stairs that require us to aim high and to work hard.** The other two indicators that have been alluded to above are the requirements for **excellence** and for **self-discipline**. But there are others also.

How do we decide which set of stairs to climb? And what is the priority if there are conflicts between these indicators? In the movie, Indiana Jones and the Last Crusade, the Grail

Knight says "But, choose wisely." **We must wisely choose the correct stairs to climb.** But, in order to find out how to wisely choose the right sets of stairs, you must continue to read the rest of this book.

CHAPTER 3

INTEGRITY

President and 1915 West Point graduate Dwight D. Eisenhower said, "The supreme quality for leadership is unquestionably integrity. Without it, no real success is possible, no matter whether it is on a section gang, a football field, in an army, or in an office." At the US Military Academy (West Point) he had learned the importance of integrity through instruction and enforcement of the West Point Honor Code which is, "A cadet will not lie, cheat, steal, or tolerate those who do." Honor and integrity have been the foundation of West Point since its founding in 1802.

Similarly, when the US Naval Academy (Annapolis) was founded in 1845, it would focus on the importance of integrity through instruction and enforcement of an honor code. When President Eisenhower signed the law that authorized the US Air Force Academy on April 1st, 1954, it was clear that USAFA would also teach integrity and would enforce an honor code. Enforcement at all three Academies means that one's failure to follow the Honor Code would result in dismissal. USAFA's Honor Code is, "We will not lie, steal, or cheat, nor tolerate among us anyone who does."

In August of 1961, at the completion of the eight weeks of Basic Cadet Summer our class received our shoulder boards, which indicated that we were Fourth-class Cadets. We were no longer Basic Cadets—we were now full-fledged USAFA Cadets—although we were still "Doolies" for another nine months. During those eight weeks of training, we had undergone intensive physical, military and ethics training.

The first week we were given a small three by five inch Air Force Academy Cadet handbook called <u>Contrails</u>. It contained much information about USAFA and about the Air Force, and it also contained a section on required fourth-class knowledge. This was to be our Doolie "Bible" for the next year, and we would be required to memorize large sections of it.

During Basic Cadet Summer we attended classes on topics covering military and Air Force history. Frequently those classes discussed exemplars—individuals who, through their actions, showed a commitment to integrity, duty and excellence. Those exemplars were then re-visited when we attended classes on ethics and the Honor Code. We learned the importance of integrity for both a leader and a follower, and we learned the importance of integrity for the organization. This organized training, education and practical experience would continue through all four years at USAFA and would be reinforced by both positive and negative experiences over the rest of my life.

Integrity is one of the fundamental ingredients of both individual and organizational trust. No organization (military or civilian) and no relationship can successfully operate without trust. Trust that each of us and the whole organization speaks the truth, trust that each of us and the whole organization will meet our commitments to each other, to the organization and to our customers, trust that each of us and the whole organization can be counted upon to do what is right in times of extreme difficulty, and trust that each of us and the whole organization will initiate action to correct bad behavior.

Imagine two different organizations, one where there is a lack of trust between superiors, subordinates, peers and customers, and the other where there is complete trust between superiors, subordinates, peers and customers. As all organizations are imperfect, each of these is an absolute example, but in real organizations, which are, either more like the former or more like the latter, how effective will each organization be in furtherance of their mission? Which organization is most likely to fail? And in which one would you rather be a member?

Senator Alan K. Simpson said, "If you have integrity, nothing else matters. If you don't have integrity, nothing else matters." This is true for both individuals and organizations.

"We will not lie…" In class and during periods of personal instruction we discussed the importance of telling the truth, of immediately correcting misstatements. We discussed that this was important when we were in both a professional and a personal situation. We were taught the USAFA definition of "quibbling", which was to make a true statement but with the intent to hide the real truth. This also was an Honor Code violation.

Later in my professional career, I would see this often as some individuals would attempt to manipulate me or would attempt to manipulate others (including customers) with correct but incomplete information. This became one of the fundamental tests to determine in whom I could place my trust. Did they communicate to inform or did they communicate to manipulate? Did they remain silent when someone was mis-informed? If they did this to others, I expected that they would do it to me and to our customers. When I was in management, I would counsel my employees if this occurred. If not corrected, they would be dismissed.

It was also important that I enforce this standard on my own performance. But telling the truth may have tactical consequences. It may not be what the boss or the customer wants to hear. In my experience, the strategic consequences of not correctly informing the boss or the customer were always greater than the tactical consequences of providing full information.

What I had to find was a tactful way to properly inform the boss or the customer to minimize the tactical consequences, but I still had to meet this integrity of communication standard. I must enforce this standard of integrity and tactfulness on my own performance, and as a leader I must enforce this standard on the organization's performance. Albert Schweitzer said, "Truth has no special time of its own. Its hour is now—always." **We must always take the stairs that lead to speaking the truth regardless of the possible consequences.**

We also discussed another aspect of telling the truth—the importance of our word. That is the aspect of making a commitment and then meeting that commitment. Trust requires that each of us (and the whole organization) needs to do what we say and to say what we will do.

In my experience, individuals and organizations that do not pay attention to the little commitments of life and business are not generally reliable when it comes to the bigger and more difficult commitments. When someone tells me that they will meet me at 6:00 PM and they do not show up until 6:30 PM, did they tell a falsehood or did their statement have no commitment? Was it unavoidable delay or just sloppiness? By their actions, do they value their time more than my time? Were their excuses true? Did they call to say that they would be late? How often has this happened in the past? Did they plan some contingency time in their travel plans so as to arrive on time? Is this a one-time occurrence or a common problem? Being on time for a meeting could be viewed as a trivial commitment, but what does it say about that person's probable response to more important commitments?

A commitment is a promise, and as Robert W. Service said, "A promise made is a debt unpaid." I must enforce this standard on my own performance and, as a leader, upon my organization's performance. **When we make a commitment, we should deliver on that commitment, no matter how hard the stairs become.**

"We will not...steal..." Stealing is taking something that does not rightfully belong to you. Everyone agrees that robbing a bank is stealing, and most people agree that shoplifting is stealing, but what about borrowing CD's, DVD's, books or tools and not returning them, borrowing anything without asking, downloading copyrighted songs without payment, not reporting a bank error in your favor, not returning money when a cashier gives you too much change, taking office supplies home for personal use, allowing the boss to think that you deserve the credit for a job well done when it was someone else?

What about a company that uses more copies of software than their license agreement allows, uses another company's proprietary information without permission, does not correct an invoice that is in their favor? All of these are varying degrees of stealing, and all of these say a lot about you and your organization's integrity and reliability. Again, I must enforce this standard on my own performance, and, as a leader, upon my organization's performance. **When the rules say that the elevator is not ours to take, we don't take the elevator (even if the door is wide open).**

"We will not...cheat..." Cheating is not following the established rules. Cheating is taking the elevator with a "do not use" sign across the door. It is breaking the rules to obtain something that you did not earn. It is an attempt to get to a specific floor without taking a required set of stairs. Plagiarism, copying another person's work, obtaining the test in advance, cheating on your taxes, claiming a benefit that you are not entitled to, cheating at a game, taking illegal steroids, taking a procedural short cut, misreporting financial information, not following a maintenance procedure and not following a checklist are all forms of cheating. Oprah Winfrey has said, "Real integrity is doing the right thing, knowing that nobody's going to know whether you did it or not."

In my experience, a person who cheats on small items cannot be trusted on the large items. The two best examples that I have seen are individuals who cheat at golf and/or who do not pay their fair share when the dinner bill and tip are split. Plato said, "You can discover more about a person in an hour of play than in a year of conversation." These individuals only fool themselves when they think that they are getting away with it. What shortcuts will they take in the workplace when they think that no one is watching? Sophocles said, "Rather fall with honor than succeed by fraud." Again, I must live this standard myself. **When the rules say don't take the elevator shortcut, we don't take that stair-cheating elevator shortcut (even if no one will find out).**

"We will not…tolerate…" This is perhaps the hardest requirement of the Honor Code. This is the requirement that when a Cadet observes a potential violation of the Honor Code by another Cadet, he/she must report it. Failure to report an observed violation of the Honor Code is in itself an Honor Code violation. Edmund Burke said, "The only thing necessary for the triumph of evil is for good men to do nothing." What we learned as Cadets was that an organization and its members cannot tolerate a lack of integrity in either the actions of the organization or the actions of its members. The difference between "Do Cadets live by the Honor Code?" and "Does the Cadet Wing live by the Honor Code?" is whether or not Cadets enforce the Honor Code on each other and is directly related to each Cadet's intolerance of dishonorable behavior by other Cadets.

Although these requirements are important for all members of any organization, it is critical for the leadership of the organization to demonstrate, inspect and enforce integrity. Leadership sets the example. Ralph Waldo Emerson said, "If you would lift me up you must be on higher ground." What I have learned throughout my professional career is that these requirements are true for every organization. At the Air Force Academy, we learned these requirements, felt the consequences sooner than students at some universities, and matured in this dimension more quickly. Upon graduation and employment, the consequences for failure to meet these requirements would be as severe for everyone entering the workplace. Organizations and individuals who do not learn this do not survive for very long.

One only has to look at Enron, Arthur Anderson and their leadership as extreme negative examples. The consequences of a lack of integrity destroyed two companies and caused many innocent shareholders and employees to incur significant loss. Enron employee Sherron Watkins is a partial example of "We will not...tolerate..." She reported the accounting fraud to the Enron CEO and to Enron's head auditor at Arthur Anderson. But, when no action was taken, should she have gone further and resigned from the company and/or gone to the SEC? **As a member or as a leader of an organization, our duty is to insure that all members take the integrity stairs. We should**

do this even though it makes our personal stairs more difficult.

In summary, the first and most important criterion for stair-taking action is integrity. Our actions in selection of the right set of stairs and in how we climb the stairs must exhibit integrity.

1. **We must always take the stairs that lead to speaking the truth regardless of the possible consequences.** Elizabeth Cady Stanton said, "Truth is the only safe ground to stand on."

2. **When we make a commitment, we should deliver on that commitment, no matter how hard the stairs become.** Aeschylus said, "It is not the oath that makes us believe the man, but the man the oath."

3. **When the rules say that the elevator is not ours to take, we don't take the elevator (even if the door is wide open).** Immanuel Kant said, "So act that your principle of action might safely be made a law for the whole world."

4. **When the rules say don't take the elevator shortcut, we don't take that stair-cheating elevator shortcut (even if no one will find out).** President Thomas Jefferson said, "Whenever you do a thing, act as if all the world were watching."

5. **As a member or as a leader of an organization, our duty is to insure that all members take the integrity stairs. We should do this even though it makes our personal stairs more difficult.** Confucius said, "To know what is right and not do it is the worst cowardice."

Looking back now on the first two chapters, each of the five rules of stair climbing can now be stated in an ethical dimension. They are:

1. **Challenge: We must challenge ourselves to the highest standard of absolute integrity.** Albert Einstein said, "Relativity applies to physics, not ethics."

2. **Self-Assessment: We should continuously self-assess our ethical performance and continue to improve upon it.** Oliver Cromwell said, "He who stops being better stops being good."

3. **Preparation: We should start early and practice on the day-to-day ethical opportunities so that when we hit the more difficult ethical challenges we are prepared to make the right decision.** Martin Luther King Jr. said, "The time is always right to do what is right."

4. **Perseverance: We must persevere through the tough ethical problems by taking the right actions and maintaining our integrity.** General George Patton said, "Moral courage is the most valuable and usually the most absent characteristic in men."

5. **Constancy: We can never stop your integrity journey!** Joan Borysenko said, "The question is not whether we will die, but how we will live."

Integrity is the fundamental underpinning of ethical behavior. The study of Ethics can best be defined as: the study of what man ought to be, not what man is. Each of us is an imperfect being, and we need to re-commit ourselves every day to self-improvement. Every day we should remind ourselves that what we have done incorrectly in the past is no excuse for continuing to do it in the future. Socrates said, "Regard your good name as the richest jewel you can possibly be possessed of—for credit is like fire; when once you have kindled it you may easily preserve it, but if you once extinguish it, you will find it an arduous task to rekindle it again. The way to gain a good reputation is to endeavor to be what you desire to appear." **When it comes to integrity, we must take the stairs.**

CHAPTER 4

DUTY

Confederate General Robert E. Lee said, "Duty then is the sublimest (sic) word in the English language. You should do your duty in all things. You can never do more. You should never wish to do less." I believe that as a Basic Cadet, this was the second quote from our <u>Contrails</u> that we were required to learn—right after the Honor Code. As members of USAFA and members of the Air Force we were required to learn each and every one of our duties and responsibilities. In addition, as Basic Cadets, we were required to execute those duties and responsibilities with excellence and enthusiasm. Failure to learn and execute quickly would result in additional "special attention." As a result, our duty and responsibilities were very quickly learned and executed.

I am reminded of the commercials of a few years ago. The tag line was "American Express, membership has its privileges.®" The more important and relevant fact is that membership in any organization also comes with its responsibilities, duties and rules to be followed. It is only by executing those responsibilities, performing those duties and living by the rules of the organization that we assure that we will continue to be entitled to the privileges of membership.

Membership in American Express may have its privileges, but it does not have its entitlements. See how long those privileges last if we do not meet our responsibilities to pay the bill every month. When we commit to join any organization, we have committed to those duties, responsibilities and rules to be followed, and, as discussed in the preceding chapter, our integrity requires us to meet our commitments. We should not join that specific organization if we are unwilling to meet those commitments. **There is no membership without duty. Duty defines the stairs we must climb.**

Our single and most important responsibility is to understand and execute our duty commitments, to understand the organization and to understand our role in that organization.

It is not sufficient to just understand and perform our assigned tasks. The true definition of duty requires that we must understand how our tasks relate to the whole organization, so that we can smartly execute those tasks to further the organization's mission. This is the real goal of any assigned taks. This includes understanding the values of the organization, the vision, the mission, the objectives, the strategies, the policies, the procedures and the plans. In execution, our responsibility is to do our duty by living the values of the organization and executing our responsibilities consistent with those values, the vision, mission, objectives, strategies, policies, procedures and plans.

As a part of this expanded definition of duty, as each of us advances in the organization, we become responsible for developing these items within our own organization and assuring that they are consistent with the greater organization's responsibilities. We should embrace this as our expanded definition of our duty. Andrew Carnegie said, "Do your duty and a little more and the future will take care of itself."

In my experience, the most respected, successful, and influential individuals in any organization (at all levels) are those who both define and execute their duty to this expanded definition. This applies to all professions and industries. **The most respected individuals take the most difficult stairs and focus on the mission and the success of the organization as their goal.** This is not the same as making an easy job harder. Rather, their individual success comes from focusing on the mission of the organization rather than focusing on their own careers.

With each organizational, mission and task success, their individual value increases to the organization, and smart organizations reward that value—with increased duties and responsibilities and more "stairs to climb". Simply said, **as we advance in an organization, our duty increases and the stairs get more difficult.**

Now let me expand the definition of organization. To what organizations do we belong? Each "organization" comes with its duties, responsibilities and rules to follow. How about our membership in humanity, our citizenship, our church, our profession, our job, our family and our close circle of friends? Each of us also has other organizational memberships in alumni associations, civic groups, clubs, etc. Do we understand each of these in terms of our duties, responsibilities and the rules to follow, and are we doing our duty to those "organizations" to which we belong?

Our sense of duty should demand that we are committed and not just involved. There is a significant difference between the definition of involvement and commitment. As with bacon and eggs, the chicken is involved and the pig is committed. **We must make a personal stair-taking commitment of duty to <u>all</u> of the "organizations" to which we belong.**

In addition to our specifically assigned duties and responsibilities, every organization requires performance to a general set of duties that are common to all successful organizations. These general duties of each organization to which we belong are:

1. To be a team player.

2. To be civil to all members.

3. To treat others as we would wish to be treated.

4. To work for the good of the organization.

5. To support superiors, subordinates, peers, and customers.

6. To defend the organization externally.

7. To keep criticism positive and productive.

8. To keep disagreements and dissention within the organization.

9. To volunteer to take on additional duties and responsibility within the organization when the need arises.

When individual members of an organization do not meet this general set of duties, the organization will see a significant reduction in its performance. **Our general duties are as important as our specific duties. We need to take both sets of stairs.**

In my experience, individuals who do not implement their general duties listed above are not promoted and frequently leave the organization (either involuntarily or by mutual initiative). As an aside, retirement or resignation does not relieve us of our general duties and responsibilities. When I have interviewed job applicants with previous experience, those who speak ill of, or share stories from their previous organizations, have been rejected. If they did not continue to implement some of their general duties and responsibilities to their previous organizations, they would be unlikely to implement these duties and responsibilities to my organization. The rule is that, **some of our duties and responsibilities to the organization continue after retirement or resignation. The stair climbing does not stop.**

An important observation here is that our loyalty should derive from and should be a requirement of our duty, rather than our duty deriving from our loyalty. More simply put, our duty to an organization demands that we be loyal to the organization—even after we leave the organization.

In summary, the second criterion for stair-taking action is duty. Our actions in selection of the right set of stairs and in how we climb those stairs must be based on a broad and expanded definition of duty.

1. **There is no membership without duty. Duty defines the stairs we must climb.** Peter Drucker said, "Never mind your happiness; Do your duty." The most respected individuals take the most difficult stairs and focus on the mission and the success of the organization as their goal.

2. George Eliot said, **"Conscientious people are apt to see their duty in that which is the most painful course."**

3. **As we advance in an organization, our duty increases and the stairs get more difficult.** Thomas Carlyle said, "Do the duty which lies nearest to you, the second duty will then become clearer."

4. **We must make a personal stair-taking commitment of duty to all of the "organizations" to which we belong.** President Calvin Coolidge said, "Duty is not collective; it is personal."

5. **Our general duties are as important as our specific duties. We need to take both sets of stairs.** Phil Jackson said, "The strength of the team is each individual member…the strength of each member is the team."

6. **Some of our duties and responsibilities to the organization continue after retirement or resignation.**

The stair climbing does not stop. G. K Chesterton said, "We are all in the same boat in a stormy sea, and we owe each other a terrible loyalty."

Again, looking back now on the first two chapters, each of the five rules of stair climbing can now be stated in the dimension of our duty. They are:

1. <u>Challenge:</u> **We should challenge ourselves to an ever-increasing and expanded definition and a high standard of duty to all of the organizations to which we belong.** Thomas Kempis said, "Activate yourself to duty by remembering your position, who you are, and what you have obliged yourself to be."

2. <u>Self-Assessment:</u> **We should self-assess our own performance and its conformance with the values, vision, mission, strategies, policies procedures and plans of all those organizations and continue to improve upon our performance.** Marie Curie said, "You cannot hope to build a better world without improving the individuals. To that end each of us must work for his own improvement and at the same time share a general responsibility for all humanity, our particular duty being to aid those to whom we think we can be most useful."

3. <u>Preparation:</u> **We should practice doing more than expected, volunteering for additional duties and responsibilities to all of the organizations to which we belong.** Mark Twain said, "Do something every day that you don't want to do; this is the golden rule for acquiring the habit of doing your duty without pain."

4. **Perseverance: When our duties and responsibilities to the organization get particularly difficult, we must persevere and deliver the best possible performance.** John Burns said, "My duty is clear and at all costs will be done."

5. **Constancy: We can never opt out of our duty and the obligations of membership.** Sir Robert Baden-Powell said, "We never fail when we try to do our duty; we always fail when we neglect to do it."

Each of us requires a focus on both integrity and duty. Either demonstrating integrity without demonstrating duty, or demonstrating duty without demonstrating integrity will lead to failure. But what if situations arise where there are conflicts between our duty and our integrity? In ethical organizations, our responsibilities to our duty and to our integrity will almost never conflict. It is therefore particularly important that we pick only highly ethical organizations to join. Even then there will sometimes be conflict. If there is an apparent conflict, we must look for a more difficult set of stairs where we can both maintain our integrity <u>and</u> do our duty.

If we find that all stairs are blocked to do both, then we must take an even more difficult set of stairs based on our integrity. If we cannot resolve this with our immediate supervisor, this should require us to go around our immediate supervisor to resolve a conflict between duty and integrity. We must keep going up the chain of command until this conflict between duty and integrity is resolved—either by our improved understanding or by a change in direction. Our duty to the organization and both our personal integrity and the organization's integrity should demand this. Stated simply, for our duty and integrity not to conflict, we should do our duty to our integrity first.

I have personally always worked in highly ethical organizations, but there have been circumstances where the ethical consequences of decisions and actions were not fully understood. Every time I raised these issues, I received a complete explanation and concluded there was no ethical conflict, or the issues were corrected. Sometimes I went to my immediate superior and sometimes I had to appeal much higher in the chain of command. This was very stressful and painful. Whether this had consequences to my career or not was unimportant, but, in fact, the consequences were probably positive. I have seen other examples where people remained silent in similar circumstances, only to be reprimanded or fired when the organization discovered the actions and the consequences. Voltaire said, "No snowflake in an avalanche ever feels responsible." In point of fact, our silence and inaction does not relieve us of our duty to protect the organization in these cases.

But, as with the Enron example, if we escalate to the top of the organization and the ethical conflict is not resolved, then it is time for us to resign from that organization and/or find a higher authority for an appeal. Depending on the circumstances and the organization, our duty and integrity require resignation and silence or our duty and integrity require resignation and further action. But staying in the organization beyond that point is less than ethical behavior on our part.

In the spring of 2006 several retired generals criticized Secretary of Defense Donald Rumsfeld about the war in Iraq. Although I do not know all of the facts, it would appear that their duty, if they disagreed with the decisions of Secretary Rumsfeld, was first to raise those disagreements with the Secretary while they were in uniform. If not successful, their duty was to either accept the decision and not second guess it (either in or out of uniform) or appeal to the President as Commander in Chief. If they were not successful with their appeal, then they should accept the decision or resign their commission if they thought that this was somehow an integrity issue. From press reports, it would appear that they did not elevate their concerns to the Secretary of Defense, and they remained on duty.

After they retired, they felt free to critique the decisions made three years before. I believe that this is an abrogation of their duty. It doesn't matter whether Secretary Rumsfeld's decisions were correct or not. I believe that the retired generals' duty requirements were clear. These generals can't have it both ways. Either they did not meet their duty requirements while in uniform, or they bought into the decisions at the time, and they are not meeting their duty requirements out of uniform. **As with integrity, when it comes to duty, we must take the stairs.**

CHAPTER 5

EXCELLENCE

During Basic Cadet Summer, one of the military exemplars that we studied was World War I General of the Armies John J. (Black Jack) Pershing. After graduating from West Point in 1886, one of newly commissioned Second Lieutenant Pershing's first assignments was to construct an outhouse. Lieutenant Pershing decided right then and there to design and construct "...the best damn outhouse that the US Army has ever seen." The focus on integrity, duty and excellence was a hallmark of General Pershing's career.

At each point in my own career, various organizations have defined expectations relative to my performance on a spectrum from "unacceptable" to "meets minimum requirements" to "good" to "excellent". Being a Doolie at USAFA meant that the expectations could best be stated as "excellence is rigorously enforced." Less than excellent performance on any individual item would receive the immediate logical consequences of corrective action up to and including the dreaded "special attention." Being a third classman at USAFA meant that the expectations could best be stated as "excellence is demanded."

A Third Class Cadet would see deferred logical consequences of individual counseling if there was a lack of excellence over a period of time. This would also affect their military order of merit and future leadership assignments. Being a second or first classman at USAFA meant that the expectations could best be stated as "excellence is expected." Although there may be some counseling in extreme cases, the actions of the Second or First Class Cadet would be reflected in the military ranking and in their selection for leadership positions. The real logical consequences to the Cadets would be their lack of leadership experiences, which they would need in their careers, and their order of merit would a have significant effect on their assignments after graduation.

I would describe most undergraduate college programs as "excellence is expected." There are limited immediate consequences from not studying—perhaps not until the end of the semester, and the consequences of a weak degree program and/or a low grade point will not be felt until after graduation.

After graduation it seems to me that the operational model for most organizations is first, "previous documented excellence is required for selection." As an example, most Fortune 500 companies only interview graduates who have taken a relevant and difficult degree program, obtained a 3.3 grade point or better (some require 3.5 or better), and have work and leadership experience. Second, after hiring, the organizational model seems to be either "excellence is expected" and/or "excellence is rewarded." In practice, this means that each of us has to learn that we must set our own standards of excellence, and that this, in fact, is the behavior that differentiates us from the rest of the people who don't understand this.

In my experience, the logical consequences to those who set their own high standards of excellence are that they generally succeed. Those who just do the job to the "meet minimum requirements" or "good" standard experience the deferred logical consequences of their actions by not advancing. Taking the elevator or the easy approach/shortcut will not be rewarded. **We must set and execute our own high standards of excellence. We must see and climb the excellence stairs.** George Washington Carver said, "When you do the common things in life in an uncommon way, you will command the attention of the world."

But excellence is relatively easy if you have infinite time and infinite resources. Most organizations reward excellence to schedule or excellence to both schedule and budget. In then-Second Lieutenant Pershing's outhouse example, it was important that he complete the project within the schedule and budget that was authorized. The only variables of which Lieutenant Pershing had control were the amount, the quality and the creativity of his own personal effort.

This "think hard/work hard" dimension is the differentiating behavior. **We must demonstrate both excellence of thought and excellence of action by climbing both sets of stairs.** As Doolies, our performance was always measured as excellence of thought and action to a deadline. It is no different in every profession and organization. Our duty to the organization requires that if the organization thinks that something is worth doing, it is worth doing with differentiating hard work and excellence. Our duty to ourselves requires that if we think that something is worth doing ourselves, it is worth doing with differentiating hard work and excellence. Whatever tasks are left over, if we are going to do them, we should still perform them with differentiating hard work and excellence. Secretary of State Colin Powell said, "If you are going to achieve excellence in big things, you develop the habit in little matters. Excellence is not an exception, it is a prevailing attitude."

From the previous chapters, it is easy to see that excellence is required in those items that relate to our integrity and to our duty. What about those items not obviously related to integrity and duty? The simple answer comes from Aristotle who said, "We are what we repeatedly do. Excellence, then, is not an act but a habit." **If we are to be excellent when it counts, we must practice stair-climbing excellence in everything that we do.**

Each of us requires a focus on and a demonstration of integrity and duty and excellence. But what if situations arise where there are conflicts between our integrity or our duty and our personal requirements for excellence? The more that we are driven to personal excellence, the more that there can be conflict between duty to an organization's mission and excellence requirements and our personal standards of excellence. As an example, our immediate superior can say, "I need it done by Thursday. Do the best you can." In this example, let us assume that we cannot meet all of our current commitments with excellence and that a schedule change is not negotiable. This example is a conflict between personal excellence and organizational excellence.

Our duty demands that we work as hard and as smart as we can to meet both the organization's standard and our own standard of excellence, but if we can't meet both, our duty requires that we must prioritize the organizational standard. Think of a painting by Michelangelo where some of the apprentices were filling in some background material. What matters is the whole painting (the organization's excellence goals) rather than the excellence of the background (our personal excellence goals). **We must find a way to climb both the organization's and our own excellence stairs, but if we can't do both, then the organization's excellence stairs must be climbed.**

In summary, the third criterion for stair-taking action is excellence. Our actions in selection of the right set of stairs and in how we climb the stairs must be based on a search for differentiating excellence.

1. **We must set and execute our own high standards of excellence. We must see and climb the excellence stairs.** José Ortega Y Gassett said, "Excellence [is achieved] when a man or woman asks of himself more than others do."

2. **We must demonstrate both excellence of thought and excellence of action by climbing both sets of stairs.** Georges Bernanos said, "A thought which does not result in an action is nothing much, and an action which does not proceed from a thought is nothing at all."

3. **If we are to be excellent when it counts, we must practice stair-climbing excellence in everything that we do.** Napoleon Hill said, "If you cannot do great things [yet], do small things in a great way."

4. **We must find a way to climb both the organization's and our own excellence stairs, but if we can't do both, then the organization's excellence stairs must be climbed.** Ralph Waldo Emerson said, "There is always a best way of doing everything."

Again, looking back now on the first two chapters, each of the five rules of stair climbing can now be stated in the dimension of your excellence. They are:

1. **<u>Challenge:</u> We must challenge ourselves to excellence in all that we do.** Vince Lombardi said, "The quality of a person's life is in direct proportion to their commitment to excellence, regardless of their chosen field of endeavor."

2. **<u>Self-Assessment:</u> Excellence is not perfection. We must self-assess our performance in all things and continue to improve.** Publilius Syrus said, "It takes a long time to bring excellence to maturity."

3. **<u>Preparation:</u> The sooner we start, the better we will get. We should perform <u>all</u> tasks with excellence.** Thomas J. Watson said, "If you want to achieve excellence, you can get

there today. As of this second, quit doing less-than-excellent work."

4. **Perseverance:** **The more difficult the task, the more important is our commitment to excellence. We must persevere and finish all tasks with excellence.** Og Mandino said, "Remember that the most difficult tasks are consummated, not by a single explosive burst of energy or effort, but by the constant daily application of the best you have within you."

5. **Constancy:** **We can never stop your excellence journey.** We should emulate President Abraham Lincoln who said, "I do the very best I know how - the very best I can; and I mean to keep on doing so until the end."

Over and over throughout my life, I have observed many individuals whose performance could best be described as just doing the job. They do not appear to be particularly happy with their job, and they were doing nothing about it. They didn't understand that their lack of an enthusiastic drive for excellence was one of the primary causes of their unhappiness. Jessica Guidobono said, "Every job is a self-portrait of the person who did it. Autograph your work with excellence." **As with integrity and duty, when it comes to excellence, we must take the stairs.**

CHAPTER 6

SELF-DISCIPLINE

From the title of this book and some of the discussions in previous chapters the reader might come to the conclusion that I am either Amish or a Luddite. I am neither. I am not trying to put the Otis Elevator Company out of business. I am not suggesting a return to a simpler time. I am actually in favor of time and labor-saving devices. I drive a car and use the clothes washer and dryer. But let's look at these time and labor saving devices a little further. Our modern world is about convenience and efficiency. But that convenience can be a trap if it leads to sloth. The issue for each of us is what do we do with the time and energy saved?

Do we apply and invest that extra time and energy in the pursuit of goals, or do we squander that time and energy? How do we get maximum benefit from our time and energy savings and investment? As President Theodore Roosevelt said, "With self-discipline most anything is possible," but for this statement to be true, there needs to be a focus on three key factors:

1. The self-discipline must be focused and goal-oriented.

2. There must be an effectiveness of effort directed towards multiple goals at the same time.

3. We must control our impulses that would take us off of our multi-goal path.

During that first Basic Cadet summer, we were told an anecdote by the upperclassmen. They said, "When you arrive at USAFA and become a Doolie they take away all of your rights. They then proceed to give them back one at a time over the next four years as privileges." As with all humor, there is an element of truth in the statements. Remember that "duolos" is the Greek word, which means slave. Actually the Greek language has multiple words for different categories of slave. In this case, perhaps a better definition of "duolos" is indentured household servant. In ancient Greece, a child would be sold as an indentured household servant for a period of years. The servant would be subject to strong discipline and would learn the skills required within the household and learn a trade. At the end of the period of years, the servant would be released from his servitude, having acquired significant self-discipline, skills and a trade. One might conclude that not much has changed.

One part of the USAFA experience and strategy is this process of putting the Doolies under total discipline, pushing us to (and through) our pre-conceived limits and therefore proving to each of us what we were really able to accomplish. This is a part of each of the military, physical training, education, character, and leadership programs. USAFA would then gradually eliminate a large number of those discipline requirements over four years. A part of this strategy is to show the Cadets the value of discipline by showing them how much they have accomplished in their personal development while they are under discipline, and then, as some of the discipline is removed, to teach the Cadets to develop their own self-discipline.

Some of us will learn this by instruction, some by example, and some by experiences from negative consequences. This is because, as "Bum" Phillips said, "The only discipline that lasts is self-discipline." In fact, these processes exist as a part of the training for all military service, in quite a few sports, and some advanced degree programs (such as law and medicine) and they generally work. In my business experience, when individuals with previous successful military experience and/or successful sports experience such as swimming, long distance running and long distance cycling are hired, they generally exhibit this focused self-discipline that makes them successful in the workplace and in life. Cyclist Lance Armstrong is an excellent example of that self-discipline. As he has said, "Pain [from "taking the stairs"] is temporary. Quitting lasts forever."

Having goal-oriented self-discipline is all about delayed gratification. It is about having goals and defining strategies of personal investment ("stair climbing") that will lead to the accomplishment of each of our goals. It is about investing time, effort and resources <u>now</u> to accomplish future goals. It is about taking the stairs <u>now,</u> so at some future time we are at a higher floor (we never get to the top). Gary Ryan Blair said, "Self-discipline is an act of cultivation. It requires you to connect today's actions to tomorrow's results. There's a season for sowing a season for reaping. Self-discipline helps you know which is which." This "take the stairs" lesson can be stated as: **We can't stand there watching the TV on the landing. We should cultivate the self-discipline to take the stairs <u>now</u> in order to accomplish our future goals.**

To work toward one goal to the exclusion of all others and then, upon accomplishment of that one goal, to proceed to the next goal is both inherently ineffective and impractical. As our journey toward one goal will frequently take a lifetime, we must pursue all goals in parallel. To make our efforts more goal-effective, we need to first define and integrate all of our goals, strategies and tasks that we have to accomplish, and then we should analyze solutions that, via accomplishment of a task, will make progress toward two or more goals/strategies. This is not multi-tasking but rather, selecting a single task approach that satisfies multiple strategies. Multi-tasking can also help, but one task that achieves multiple strategies is even more effective. With a little practice, this can become second nature. In other words, we should look for methods that will "kill two or more birds with one stone."

Using the "take the elevator or take the stairs" decision example, from multiple goals, first I derive multiple strategies. As a set of goal/strategy examples, I have committed to attend a meeting (goal) by going from the ground floor to the third floor where the meeting will be held (strategy). I want to lose weight (goal) by getting additional daily exercise (strategy). I want to maintain a certain level of aerobic fitness (goal) by walking/climbing exercise (strategy). I want to be ready for ski season (goal) by getting my legs in shape (strategy). And I want to be neat and presentable when I attend the meeting (goal) by not working up too much of a sweat before the meeting (strategy). Can I make progress toward all of these goals by taking the stairs? The only two questions that are left to answer are: can I arrive on time if it requires additional time to take the stairs and does my current level of fitness allow me to arrive without too much sweat?

In practice, walking three floors up or four floors down is generally as fast as awaiting the arrival of, and then taking the elevator (I've timed it!), so the time saving element should not apply in those cases. Since I normally allow extra time to make sure that I meet my commitment to be on time for the meeting (chapter 4—duty) I decide to take the stairs at a pace that will keep me neat and presentable. The more I do this, the easier it becomes and the faster my pace as I take the stairs. This simple example was the trigger that caused me to see the "take the stairs" metaphor and to want to write this book. The "stair-climbing" lesson can be stated as: **We should select and take the stairs now that offer the most progress toward accomplishing our multiple future goals.**

Controlling our impulses that take us off of our goal path is perhaps the most difficult aspect of self-discipline. We can be on the right path, but if our impulses take us off that path, we will have lost ground. As the old proverb states, "The road to Hell is paved with good intentions." I am reminded of the children's board game called <u>Chutes and Ladders</u>. The objective is to roll the dice and get to the top of the board. Along the way, there are ladders that will move you up quickly toward the top of the board and chutes that will move you down quickly toward the bottom to the board. There is no skill in this game, only luck associated with the roll of the dice. In keeping with the "take the stairs" metaphor, the game of life could be called <u>Chutes, Elevators and Stairways</u>. But unlike the board game that is two-dimensional, our decisions about our multiple goals and how high we aim determine the number of dimensions to the game (and the number of dimensions to each of us).

Each of us needs to define multiple sets of goals. We should define challenging and laudable goals in <u>all</u> of the following areas: our high aspirations relative to our career, our multiple friendships (discussed in the next chapter), our lifestyle, our financial security, our health, our service to others, our enjoyment of life, and our legacy. Each of these goals has the potential to support or to conflict with the other goals. Our challenges will be to define high goals in each of these categories, to prioritize each of these goals, and to maximize the accomplishment of all of our goals.

Unlike the board game, which is based completely on luck, as we work through the game of life, we have decisions to make. In life, we may not be able to control the basic roll of the dice on the main path (our lifeline), but we do have control of our lives to the extent that we can decide to take or not take any available chutes, elevators or stairways. The elevators and stairways represent those items as described in the previous chapters. The chutes represent those items that take us away from our goals (e. g. the chocolate sundae if we are trying to maintain our weight or to lose weight). Since we should not be victims of chance, we can and should take charge of all of our decisions.

In order to come out ahead in the game of life, **we must understand the fundamental differences between stairways, elevators and chutes and choose wisely**. As discussed in preceding chapters, we should first decide to look for stairways that lead to our goal accomplishment. When we are presented with a decision to take a stairway, we need to analyze this decision in terms of its positive benefit to all of our goals as described in the chapters above. When we are presented with the decision to take a very fun and enjoyable chute, we again analyze it in terms of the negative effect on all of our goals and what additional stairways that we will have to take to make up that impact. The longer the distance that we would drop on the chute, the more likely that we should reject it.

Remember that one of our life's goals is our enjoyment. We must select enjoyment that has positive impact (or at least minimal negative impact) on our other goals. **When we are on the stairs and working toward our goals, we must not be distracted by the pretty signs that lead to fun chutes that drop us down a floor or more.** When we are presented with a decision to take an elevator, as described in the chapters above, we should probably reject it.

Unlike the board game, the game of life has an unknown time limit, although our goals related to health can influence that time limit. Throughout our individual game, we won't play perfectly. Sometimes we will ignore stairways that we should have taken, sometimes we will take chutes that we should have rejected and sometimes we will have taken those elevators that we should have rejected. Each time we do make one of those decisions, we should assess the consequences and learn to do better the next time.

Now let's talk about some specific examples. Use of a credit card with a deferred payment is an apparent elevator that appears to get us to a specific purchase goal sooner, but not only do we still have to climb the set of stairs related to the cost of the purchase, but you also have to climb an additional set of stairs for the interest payments. A credit card is really a downward chute that takes us further away from our financial security goals. At 18% interest rate on a credit card, the purchase of one flight of stairs requires the later climbing of two flights of stairs (assuming minimum payment). In fact, saving/investing at any positive return results in a reduction in the number of stairs in the flight of stairs. I did not learn this early in my life (to my eventual dismay). I had to climb a many stairs to eliminate my large credit card debt. The better strategy is financial self-discipline and impulse control—to take the stairs by saving money and paying cash for the items that we need.

Another example is our health, exercise and diet goals. To live healthier and longer, current science tells us that our strategy must be diet (the right foods) exercise, (aerobic, strength and flexibility) and weight control (caloric intake). As we grow older, the more important this becomes, but the habits of a lifetime are difficult to change, so it behooves us to start early. Charles Noble said, "First we make our habits, then our habits make us." Perhaps there is no area that requires more self-discipline and more control of our impulses.

Why is it that it is easy to eat a whole bag of potato chips, but that is unlikely to happen with a family size bowl of broccoli? Is that because broccoli is a "take the stairs" food while potato chips are a "take a chute" food? This is an area where I must personally admit insufficient success. I have tried every "elevator" diet imaginable—from Atkins to the Zone and every letter in between. The good news is that I have probably lost 500 pounds while on those diets since I graduated from USAFA. The bad news is that I have gained 550 pounds while not on those diets. What I must do is change my whole lifestyle so that I am working toward these goals every day by climbing the stairs, not believing in elevators, and avoiding the chutes.

Candidly, I am making some significant progress in my lifestyle changes; however I need to change faster, because as I get older, much more progress is necessary. I feel somewhat like the baseball player Mickey Mantle who said, "If I knew I was going to live this long, I'd have taken better care of myself." For each of us, our self-discipline in this area has to be in place and increase faster than our own individual aging process, and we need to accomplish this via prediction, rather than observing the negative results as a trigger to our action.

The last example that I will discuss is the broad category of addictions. These could be gambling, alcohol, sex, smoking, drugs, video games, the Internet or food (and many others). In general, an addiction can be defined as a compulsive psychological and/or physiological dependency. The compulsive and all consuming aspect of the addiction is a dangerous chute that takes us far away from our other goals, and the specific addiction may have other health and legal consequences. Mike Drabant has said, "Just like Superman, each of us has our potential 'kryptonite'." We must all be very wary of any enjoyment that threatens addiction. The ancient Greeks believed in moderation. Each of us must find that moderation and avoid the chutes that lead to excess.

In summary, the fourth criterion for stair-taking action is self-discipline. Our actions in selection of the right set of stairs and in how we climb the stairs must be based on goal-focused self-discipline.

1. **We can't stand there watching the TV on the landing. We should cultivate the self-discipline to take the stairs now in order to accomplish our future goals.** Jesse Owens said, "We all have dreams. But in order to make dreams come into reality, it takes an awful lot of determination, dedication, self-discipline, and effort."

2. **We should select and take the stairs now that offer the most progress toward accomplishing our multiple future goals.** Peter Drucker said, "Efficiency is doing things right; effectiveness is doing the right things."

3. **We must understand the fundamental differences between stairways, elevators and chutes and choose wisely.** David Starr Jordan said, "Wisdom is knowing what to do next; virtue is doing it."

4. **When we are on the stairs and working toward our goals, we must not be distracted by the pretty signs that lead to fun chutes that drop us down a floor or more.** Sir

Edmund Hillary said, "It is not the mountain we conquer but ourselves."

Again, looking back now on the first two chapters, each of the five rules of stair climbing can now be stated in the dimension of your self-discipline. They are:

1. **Challenge: We are in charge of your lives. We must challenge ourselves to make smart decisions based on our goals and based on self-discipline.** Leonardo da Vinci said, "One can have no smaller or greater mastery than mastery of oneself."

2. **Self-Assessment: We all make mistakes. These are not failures if we do not continue to repeat them. We must self-assess our performance in terms of our goals and our self-discipline as it affects our goals and continue to improve in both.** Grenville Kleiser said, "By constant self-discipline and self-control you can develop greatness of character."

3. **Preparation: The sooner that we start, the better we will get. We should perform with self-discipline all tasks immediately at hand.** Lucius Annaeus Seneca said, "We should every night call ourselves to an account; what infirmity have I mastered today? What passions opposed? What temptation resisted? What virtue acquired? Our vices will abort of themselves if they be brought every day to the shrift."

4. **Perseverance: We should never make the decision on the difficulty of the stairway or the enjoyment of the chute without considering the importance to our goals. We should pass this test if we truly want to accomplish our**

goals. President Harry S. Truman said, "In reading the lives of great men, I found that the first victory they won was over themselves...self-discipline with all of them came first."

5. **Constancy: There will be new challenges and new temptations. We will never complete our self-discipline journey.** Lucius Annaeus Seneca said, "What you think is the top, is only a step."

I don't believe that self-discipline can ever conflict with integrity, duty and excellence. In fact, in order to live with integrity, do your duty and do everything with excellence, self-discipline is a key ingredient. Plato said, "The first and best victory is to conquer self." **In order to master self-discipline, we must take the stairs, reject the elevators and avoid the chutes.**

CHAPTER 7

FRIENDSHIP

English poet John Donne said, "No man is an island…" Everyone is or should be our "friend" (or "Friend", or "FRIEND" or "FRIEND" or "**FRIEND**" or "**FRIEND**"). Each of us must remember the golden rule that is a part of most religions, but it has a foundation in the study of ethics and is the basis of English Common Law. It is called the ethic of reciprocity. Simply stated, we should treat everyone else as we would wish to be treated. Ralph Waldo Emerson said, "The only way to have a friend is to be one." But the question becomes how do we select our friends—and how do they select us?

President George Washington said, "Be courteous to all, but intimate with few, and let those few be well tried before you give them your confidence. True friendship is a plant of slow growth, and must undergo and withstand the shocks of adversity before it is entitled to the appellation." At every depth of friendship, to take on a friendship is to take on a mutual duty and obligation.

In "stair-taking" words, **duty and obligation represent the set of stairs which each of us must be willing to climb to develop and maintain each friendship**. The deeper the friendship becomes, the fewer the number of friends, and the deeper the duty and obligation becomes. Again, in "stair-taking" words, **the deeper the friendship, the steeper the stairs that each of us must be willing to climb to maintain the friendship.** I would agree with the unknown author who said, "You don't make friends, you earn them."

In practice, the depth of friendships extends across a continuum, and friendships continue to individually move across that continuum, either getting deeper or shallower over long periods of time. However, in order to have a meaningful discussion, I am going to first describe five different and very broad points on that continuum as five different levels of friendship and then later discuss development, maintenance and movement along the continuum.

Each of our individual family members can be defined at one of these levels in this process with different family members placed at different levels. As an example, the cousin that you haven't seen for five years will be at a different level than your spouse or sibling. The different levels of friendship are:

1. "friend": This level is best labeled as "acquaintance." The order of magnitude over a lifetime is tens of thousands of

acquaintances. As members of humanity, we each have a duty and an obligation to everyone to be polite and to behave with respect.

In this case, a failure of the other individual to do his or her duty does not relieve us of our duty to civility and respect. James D. Miles said, "You can easily judge the character of a man by how he treats those who can do nothing for him." This is also true of a superior's treatment of subordinates at the next level defined below.

2. "Friend": This level is best labeled as "co-worker" or "teammate" and can include superior/subordinate relationships. The order of magnitude over a lifetime is thousands of co-workers and teammates.

As the friendship deepens to this level, we take on additional obligations (without ever giving up the previous obligations). If we are members of the same organization (note the expanded definition of both "organization" and duty in chapter 4), our common duty causes us to have interlocking obligations. This requires us to support each other in support of our joint and individual duties. Yogi Berra said, "When you're part of a team, you stand up for your teammates. Your loyalty is to them. You protect them through good and bad, because they'd do the same for you." Again, in this case, a failure of another member of the team to meet their duties and responsibilities does not relieve us of our duties and responsibilities to that member because of our over-riding duties and responsibilities to our common team/organization.

However, this group does divide into two groups: people we want to work with and can trust, and people we don't want to work with and can't trust. When our duty requires that we have to work with the latter, we must execute our duty. Said another way, duty to a teammate derives from duty to the organization.

3. "FRIEND": This level is best labeled as "true friend". The order of magnitude over a lifetime is hundreds of true friends although at any one time in our life the order of magnitude is tens of true friends.

    At this level of deeper friendship, our joint duty requires us to support each other in accomplishment of both our joint <u>and</u> our individual goals. There must also be mutual understanding and agreement that both parties are at this level of friendship. The friendship revolves around time willingly spent together, joint trust, sharing of problems, sharing of advice and some amount of mutual agreement to be this level of friendship. This mutual agreement is usually not stated but rather a result of observation, interaction and mutual build-up of trust over a long period of time.

    Will Miller defines these friends as, "…refrigerator friends— those people with whom we feel enough comfort to help ourselves to the food in their refrigerators [without asking]." At this point it is perhaps better said that duty to a true friend derives from shared trust and shared loyalty. But we need to be <u>very selective</u> with this level and higher level of friendships. Confucius said, "Have no friends not equal to yourself." I believe that Confucius' statement refers to this level of friendship and higher levels. I also believe that he did not mean equality in terms of our position, our wealth, our age or our experience. I believe that he was referring to our character. In reading his other writings, and consistent with the ancient Japanese proverb, "When the character of a man is not clear to you, look at his friends." I believe that Confucius meant this in terms of the elements of character described in previous chapters (laudable goals, work ethic, integrity, duty, excellence, and self-discipline), and this requires observation and interaction over a long period of time.

The best and true friendships are those where each of us is improved by the friendship over time. **Our true and close friends and soul mates must have stairway alignment with us with respect to goals, work ethic, integrity, duty, excellence, self-discipline and joint trust. We each must be very selective as to whom we select regardless of our loneliness.**

4. **"FRIEND"**: This level is best labeled as "close personal friend." The order of magnitude over a lifetime is tens of close personal friends, although at any one time the number is probably less than ten close personal friends.

   This level of friendship revolves around time willingly spent together, joint trust, sharing of problems, sharing of advice and a <u>willingness to sacrifice for each other.</u> This is a broad category based on the problems of one friend becoming the problems of the other friend and based on how much sacrifice each friend is willing to make for the other.

   In order for this level of friendship and above to be successful, there must be some psychic and/or sacrifice equality in the relationship, and there must be mutual agreement to be at this level of friendship. Again, this mutual agreement is usually not stated but rather a result of observation, interaction, and actual sacrifice for each other. It also means that there will be a mutual build-up of shared trust and shared loyalty over a long period of time. When Aristotle said, "Misfortune shows those who are not really friends", I believe that he was saying "…those who are not really close personal friends" because we discover that they do not feel our pain from misfortune and are unwilling to sacrifice for us.

5. "**FRIEND**": This level is best labeled as "soul-mate." At some level of depth in a relationship we are willing to sacrifice almost everything and perhaps even our life for these friends or family members.

This is not to be confused with the soldier who falls on the grenade to save his friends. In this case, he is probably acting on a higher duty to the whole team rather than to individual friendship. Also, although we might be willing to sacrifice our life for our young children, I do not put them in this category. Young children are our duty and responsibility, but they are not our friends at this level, as there is not yet an equal obligation for them to sacrifice for us. They would probably fit in the "teammate" category as members of the family team. I will discuss children in much more depth in the next chapter.

This category of relationship is the ultimate level of friendship and is a very narrow category. This level of friendship revolves around our lives willingly spent together, joint trust, sharing of problems, sharing of advice and a willingness to sacrifice everything for each other, and is based upon love. This level of friendship will take significant time and effort to jointly develop. An example of this commitment is the standard wedding vows, "...for better, for worse, for richer, for poorer, in sickness and in health, to love and to cherish, 'till death do us part." Needless to say, making this commitment creates a set of serious duties and responsibilities, and our integrity demands that we do not make this commitment quickly or lightly.

We must be both open and on our guard in all relationships. In particular we must be on guard against apparent friendliness with the intention to take advantage of our friendliness. By taking small steps in relationships, over a period time, we can determine whether we are being manipulated. These "users" should be avoided. Of course, our own integrity requires us not to manipulate anyone else. I should add a discussion on the subject of sexual attraction as the basis for relationships. The "on guard" discussion above certainly applies.

Mutual sexual attraction may be the basis to start a friendship, but the fundamental questions of character alignment to include goals (including fun together), work ethic, integrity, duty, excellence and self-discipline should, at least partially, be answered before the relationship advances. Sexual attraction will pale in the face of differing views on goals, work ethic, integrity, duty, excellence, self-discipline and the difficult task of making relationships work.

Relationships that start with sex and then only later answer these questions frequently fail. Sex prior to a strong relationship based on the above is a chute (as described in the previous chapter) which takes us away from our strong relationship goals, while sex, after establishing a broad and deep relationship based on the above, is a joint stairway to a deeper, more fulfilling relationship. Self-discipline should prevail, and sex should be the expression of an existing deep relationship. **There are no elevator short cuts to deep friendships. The stairways of mutual friendship, mutual respect, mutual trust, mutual sacrifice, and, eventually, mutual love must be climbed together.**

Now, I'd like to start the relationship development and maintenance discussion with a fishing metaphor. When you go fly fishing for 20-pound fish with 15-pound test line, it takes a significant amount of patience and skill to get the fish in the boat. The first thing you do is set the hook by a quick short tug--not too hard, or you will break the line. Once the hook is set, then you need to try to move the fish toward the boat by constant light pressure and by taking up the slack in the line whenever the fish moves toward the boat.

When the fish swims away from the boat, then you put some tension on the line, but you don't use too much tension, or you will break the line. After a while, the fish will get tired and will find it easier to swim toward the boat. If you are an outstanding fisherman, you can sing to the fish and get it to jump into the boat. That's when you reel in the line. If the fish changes its mind and starts to run again, you let out the line and let it run.

We cannot unilaterally control our friendships. In every relationship, each of us is both part-fisherman and part-fish. A part of each of us wants the relationship for the satisfaction that it can bring and is willing to pay the "stair-climbing" price of all of the hard work to make the relationship be successful. A part of us is afraid of the relationship because of the responsibility and possible hurt and just wants to swim away. But English author

Samuel Johnson said, "If a man does not make new acquaintances as he advances through life, he will soon find himself alone. A man…should keep his friendships in constant repair." To do this we must keep our fishing line constantly in the water, but as discussed, we should be looking for quality fish. At each level of friendship, if we want to go to a deeper level, we must, by our actions, show that deeper level of commitment. Like the Good Samaritan, we must do more than expected if we wish to deepen any relationship.

At any point in a relationship we each may feel more like the fisherman or more like the fish. The possibilities are two fish connected by a fishing line, two fishermen or a fisherman and a fish. The tensile strength of the fishing line represents the strength of the relationship on the continuum described above. As with the parsing above, two "friends" are joined by a one-pound test line, while two "**FRIENDS**" are joined by a 10,000-pound test line. The disconnects that can happen in any relationship between two friends are fisherman/fish disconnects. Someone is more the fisherman and someone is more the fish. These roles can reverse for each different disconnect, or both friends can be fish. It is always changing in strength (increasing and decreasing).

Put more than 15 pounds of pressure on a 15-pound test line, and it will break. No matter how badly you want the fish in the boat (a specific disconnect), you have to take your time and not exceed the tensile strength of the fishing line. Sometimes you can get a temporary acquiescence. But even if there is a temporary acquiescence, there will be resentment to having been forced which will ultimately do harm to the relationship. This is a lot like Zen. To try too hard to achieve the ends is to lose it.

Rather, take each step as it comes. Good friends will treat disconnects as temporary tactical issues to work through together (each will be fishermen). **Good friends will help keep each other focused on each of our goals, our work ethic, our integrity, our duty, our excellence, our self-discipline and maintaining high quality friendships.** The quality of the journey together is the real friendship—not the destination. Robert M. Pirsig said, "Sometimes it's a little better to travel than to arrive."

In summary, the fifth criterion for stair-taking action is quality friendships. Our actions in selection of the right set of stairs and in how we climb the stairs must be based on maintaining quality friendships.

1. **Duty and obligation represent the set of stairs that each of us must be willing to climb to develop and maintain each friendship.** James Francis Byrnes said, "Friendship without self interest is one of the rare and beautiful things in life."

2. **The deeper the friendship, the steeper the stairs that each of us must be willing to climb to maintain the friendship.** Charles Alexander Eastman said, "Friendship is held to be the severest test of character. It is easy, we think, to be loyal to a family and clan, whose blood is in your own veins. Love between a man and a woman is founded on the mating instinct and is not free from desire and self-seeking. But to have a friend and to be true under any and all trials is the mark of a man!"

3. **Our true and close friends and soul mates must have stairway alignment with us with respect to goals, work**

ethic, integrity, duty, excellence, self-discipline and joint trust. **We each must be very selective as to whom we select regardless of our loneliness.** G. Randolf said, "Truly great friends are hard to find, difficult to leave, and impossible to forget."

4. **There are no elevator short cuts to deep friendships. The stairways of mutual friendship, mutual respect, mutual trust, mutual sacrifice, and, eventually, mutual love must be climbed together.** Bronwyn Polson said, "Whoever says Friendship is easy has obviously never had a true friend!"

5. **Good friends will help keep each other focused on each of our goals, our work ethic, our integrity, our duty, our excellence, our self-discipline and maintaining quality friendships.** Henry Ford said, "My best friend is the one who brings out the best in me."

Again, looking back now on the first two chapters, each of the five rules of stair climbing can now be stated in the dimension of your friendships. They are:

1. <u>**Challenge:**</u> **We must challenge ourselves to be open to relationships, to be a friend to everyone, and to maintain high standards for deep friendships.** James M Barrie said, "Always be a little kinder than necessary."

2. <u>**Self-Assessment:**</u> **We each need to self-assess all of our relationships and our contribution and performance within those relationships.** Ausonius said, "Forgive many things in others; nothing in yourself."

3. <u>**Preparation:**</u> **The sooner we start developing a commitment to broad and deep relationships, the better**

we will become at being a friend and the more quality we will have in our friendships. President Abraham Lincoln said, "The better part of one's life consists of his friendships."

4. **Perseverance:** **We should fight to keep each valued friendship by being willing to work together to solve tactical issues and support each other through any difficulty.** Ben Johnson said, "True friendship consists not in the multitude of friends, but in their worth and value."

5. **Constancy:** **Our door should always be open to new old friends, new friends, and even past friends. Life is too short to waste any opportunity to improve our friendships.** Edward Everett Hale said, "The making of friends, who are real friends, is the best token we have of a man's success in life."

Throughout each of our lives, there will be conflict between our relationships and our goals, work ethic, integrity, duty, excellence and self-discipline. If we have successfully selected our deeper friendships based on a sharing of those common characteristics, then each of us has a better understanding of the importance of those characteristics and is willing to work with the other when there is conflict. The priority must be integrity first, duty second, excellence third, self-discipline always and friendships aligned.

The most common conflict is duty to work interfering with time for the friendship. If there is understanding and alignment, the friend understands the priority and accepts it. If there is not, then there will be major issues in the relationship. Similarly, in the relationship dimension, individuals fall into the three categories: "take the stairs" people, "look for the elevator" people and "stay on the same floor" people. 'Take the elevator" people expect relationships to be easy and get off at the next floor at the first sign of difficulty.

If two "take the elevator" people get married, they will not recognize that they have just entered the bottom of a stairwell. A successful marriage will take hard work. If they don't learn this, they will get off at the second floor at the divorce court. "Stay on the same floor" people do not understand the need to work hard, grow and change together. "Take the stairs" people know that the stairs are hard work and help each other up the stairs. They jointly accomplish incremental growth goals and celebrate each flight that they climb together. As we go through life, we will earn our deepest friendships on the stairs. **As with integrity, duty, excellence and self-discipline, when it comes to friendships, we must take the stairs.**

CHAPTER 8

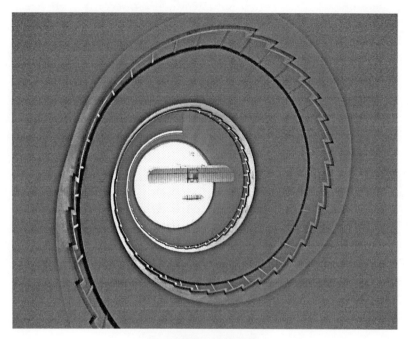

CAREER

Rather than starting this discussion about career, I would like to start the discussion with a definition of personal success. Our career is an important component of our personal success. First, let me define success as a lifetime of personal fulfillment. This sounds deceptively simple. The difficult and complex part is achieving this over a lifetime. What provides personal fulfillment in our 20's will be different in our 30's, in our 40's, in our 50's etc. How can we make the right decisions and take the right actions which will allow for our normal growth and change, while maximizing our future fulfillment as we grow and change?

Will a 100% focus on our career and our advancement keep us personally fulfilled over our lifetime? Will 100% focus on our self-development keep us personally fulfilled over our lifetime? Will a 100% focus on self-enjoyment with our career viewed merely as a way to finance self-enjoyment keep us personally fulfilled over your lifetime? Will a 100% focus on friendships, marriage and family with our career viewed merely as a way to finance relationships, marriage and family keep us personally fulfilled over our lifetime? It is only by keeping these four areas of focus in relative balance that we can achieve fulfillment over our lifetime.

This relative balance does not mean equality but rather equilibrium. This equilibrium will change as we go through life. As discussed in previous chapters, early investment in each of our life goals will be fundamental to our success. One of the first questions that we should answer is what profession and what career do we choose? Whatever we choose, it should be a profession and a career that gives us pride, that will provide challenge, satisfaction and enjoyment, and, as we grow and change, that will grow and change with us. Said in stair-taking language, **we should select a career that will give us satisfying stairs to climb over our lifetimes.**

Once we have selected our career, how much focus should we put into it? After the previous chapters there is not much left to say. If we focus on our challenging and laudable life goals, our work ethic, our integrity, our duty, our excellence, our self-discipline and our friendships, then our career will take care of itself. We must never sacrifice our life goals, our integrity, our duty, our excellence, our self-discipline or our quality friendships for our career; although we must understand that our career will play a very important part of our life goals. Helen Hayes said, "My mother drew a distinction between achievement and success. She said that 'achievement is the knowledge that you have studied and worked hard and done the best that is in you. Success is being praised by others, and that's nice, too, but not as important or satisfying. Always aim for achievement and forget about success.'"

As was discussed in the chapter on duty, this focus on achievement should be on achieving the mission of the organization. In my experience, people who focus on their own career as a priority over the achievement of the organization become branded as "climbers", and they quickly become identified as such, and just as quickly they lose the trust of subordinates (usually first), then peers and superiors. They may make some tactical progress with this approach, but this lack of trust usually derails their career. This prioritization of career over mission is perhaps best described as one of these elevators that appear to be short cuts but do not work. **While climbing the career stairs, we should keep our focus on our integrity, our duty, our excellence, our self-discipline, and our friendships and our career will take care of itself.**

Even when we have the right attitude and mission focus, we will sometimes feel dissatisfaction with our career progress. The questions that we should ask ourselves are as follows: Have we selected the right career? If we have selected the right career, is our current organization providing the right course? If we have selected the right career and our current organization is providing the right course, is our dissatisfaction only with the speed of our growth and/or advancement? I will deal with each of these questions one at a time.

The first question is, "Have we selected the right career?" All careers have a basic "price of entry" where we develop the skills and prove that we have the skills to be a member, a "price of internship" where we develop the experience and prove that we have the experience to be a member, and a "price of continuity" where we continue to improve and prove that we should continue to be a member. During my Basic Cadet Summer, I kept asking myself if I had selected the right career. At that point, I was in the "price of entry" phase of my career. I had no new information relative to the Air Force career itself. All I had was the discovery that the "price of entry" was steep.

If I was unwilling to pay this price, what career would I select in its place and what would be its "price of entry?" If I changed careers, would I again be surprised by the magnitude of the new "price of entry?" Was I looking for the "elevator" career—the career that would give me pride, that would provide challenge, satisfaction and enjoyment, and, as I grew and changed, would it grow and change with me, but have little or no "price of entry"? Well, as Robert A. Heinlein has said, "TANSTAAFL. There ain't no (sic) such thing as a free lunch." The only question to be asked is "Is the current and future pain worth the current and future pain."

For a career to engender pride of accomplishment, be challenging, satisfying and enjoyable, and grow and change as we grow and change, that career will require a significant number of stairs to climb—in the price of entry, the price of internship and the price of continuity (our duty).

If we don't continue with the career that we have selected, then what else would we do? This sort of life-changing decision should be made <u>very</u> carefully and with non-emotional analysis. If we are going to consider a change in career, we should not be "running from" our current career selection, but rather we should be "running to" another career with open eyes about the prices to be paid.

The second question is, "Are our life goals and our career compatible with our current organization?" **Our career success will be through organizational success. We must pick the organizations to which we belong as carefully as we pick our close friends. These organizations should be aligned with our laudable goals, be aligned and reward our work ethic, our integrity, our duty, our excellence, and our self-discipline and be aligned with our friendship model of civility, trust and respect.** This compatibility and alignment should not be viewed as the current short-term assignment but rather the overall expected succession of assignments over a period of years. With any career, there will be necessary tasks that will be less enjoyable and may not be directly related to our vision of our career.

The "I don't do windows" attitude is an abrogation our duty and responsibility to the organization. Also, the more narrowly we define our career, the less flexible and the less successful we will be. No task should be beneath us if it is critical to the success of the mission. If we are looking at a continuing series of future assignments over the next few years that do not match the proper expectations of life goals and our career, then we should be looking for a new organization.

The last question to be asked is, "Are we growing and/or advancing fast enough?" Our real questions should be to ourselves. Are we working hard and smart enough, are we doing our full duty, are we demonstrating excellence in everything that we do, and are we a good friend to everyone? **If we are not satisfied with our career progress, we should first look at our own performance.** We are building invisible capital, every day that we do our best in each of these dimensions. For us to look for a new organization that will pay us more or advance us faster is to lose that capital and to look for an elevator to success.

In the process of reviewing many resumes, I have seen more than a few where the individual had changed jobs every two years or so. It would appear that they were looking for career success by frequently moving from company to company. Needless to say, I was not interested in hiring them. Those individuals who change organizations too frequently are either bad at picking the right organization, undecided about their career path or expecting too much career progress for too little work. They are probably best described as "elevator people."

In summary, the sixth criterion for stair-taking action is our career. Our selection of the right set of stairs and how we climb them should be based on selecting the right career, the right organization and sticking with those decisions.

1. **We should select a career that will give us satisfying stairs to climb over our lifetime.** George Eliot said, "The best augury of a man's success in his profession is that he thinks it the finest in the world."

2. **While climbing the career stairs, we should keep our focus on our integrity, our duty, our excellence, our self-discipline, and our friendships and our career will take care of itself.** Henry David Thoreau said, "Be true to your work, your word, and your friend."

3. **For a career to engender pride of accomplishment, be challenging, satisfying and enjoyable, and grow and change as we grow and change, that career will require a significant number of stairs to climb—in the price of entry, the price of internship and the price of continuity (our duty).** Robert Frost said, "The difference between a job and a career is the difference between forty and sixty hours a week."

4. **Our career success will be through organizational success. We must pick the organizations to which we belong as carefully as we pick our close friends. These organizations should be aligned with our laudable goals, be aligned and reward our work ethic, our integrity, our duty, our excellence, our self-discipline and be aligned with our friendship model of civility, trust and respect.** C. Wright Mills said, "The life-fate of the modern individual depends not only upon the family into which he was born or which he enters by marriage, but increasingly upon the corporation in which he spends the most alert hours of his best years."

5. **If we are not satisfied with our career progress, we should first look at our own performance.** Horace said, "No man ever reached to excellence in any one art or profession without having passed through the slow and painful process of study and preparation."

Again, looking back on the first two chapters, each of the five rules of stair climbing can now be stated in the dimension of your career. They are:

1. **Challenge: We must challenge ourselves to pick a rewarding, satisfying and fulfilling career.** Norman Vincent Peale said, "Nothing of great value in life comes easily."

2. **Self-Assessment: We each need to continuously self-assess our performance with respect to our career objectives and make necessary improvements in ourselves.** J. Paul Getty said, "The individual who wants to reach the top in business must appreciate the might and force of habit. He must be quick to break those habits that can break him—and hasten to adopt those practices that will become the habits that help him achieve the success he desires."

3. **Preparation: Every career requires preparation. The sooner we develop a commitment to our career goals, understand the "price of entry", the "price of internship" and the "price of continuity" and start climbing those stairs, the more progress that we will make.** Miguel de Cervantes said, "To be prepared is half the victory."

4. **Perseverance: Whatever career you choose, there will be significant difficulties to overcome. Not all will be known in advance. To achieve success, you must persevere through each and every difficulty.** B. C. Forbes said, "History has demonstrated that the most notable winners usually encountered heartbreaking obstacles before they triumphed. They won because they refused to become discouraged by their defeats."

5. **Constancy:** **In any career, we must keep your skills current, and keep our enthusiasm and effort continuous.** Arthur Ashe said, "Success is a journey, not a destination. The doing is often more important than the outcome."

   As with integrity, duty, excellence, self-discipline, and friendships, when it comes to our career, we must take the stairs.

CHAPTER 9

CHILDREN

As parents we take on a set of awesome duties and responsibilities. We have responsibilities to our children to love them, to protect them and to provide for them, to teach and prepare them for the real world, to help them achieve their independence and, perhaps most importantly, to help them develop their character. As they grow up, these objectives can potentially conflict. When they are born, our first and most important responsibility to our children is to provide protection.

As they grow up, as parents we must walk a line between protecting our children and preparing them for the bumps and bruises of the real world. Ann Landers said, "What the vast majority of American children need is to stop being pampered, stop being indulged, stop being chauffeured, and stop being catered to. In the final analysis it is not what you do for your children but what you have taught them to do for themselves that will make them successful human beings." We must learn to provide less and less service and protection for our children and allow our children to become more responsible and more independent as they grow older.

Our first and most important responsibility as a parent is to love our children, but there is a difference between loving our children and loving everything they do. Bill Cosby said, "Even though your kids will consistently do the exact opposite of what you're telling them to do, you have to keep loving them just as much." As we both love and discipline your children that love will not always be (apparently) reciprocated. **We must climb both the love and the discipline stairs for our children.**

Our second responsibility as a parent is to prepare our children for the real world. Children must develop both the necessary skills for life, and they must experience the natural and logical consequences of their own actions at a very early age. The necessary skills come from education and hard work. As an aside, I disagree with the practice of naming advanced or accelerated programs "gifted and talented" programs. This implies that the selection criterion and what we value is based on talent rather than demonstrated success through hard work.

Our children's learning comes from the natural and logical consequences of their own actions. As defined by Rudolf Dreikurs in the book Children: the Challenge, an example of a natural consequence is gravity. If you run too fast, you may trip and fall and skin your knees. An example of a logical consequence is a family rule. If you put your clothes in the hamper, they get washed. If you don't put them in the hamper, they don't get washed. But these natural and logical consequences must be age-appropriate. Each natural and logical consequence of life is an opportunity for an incredible teaching and learning moment. I have seen parents of school age children, when there are issues at school, come immediately to the defense of their "perfect" child. This sort of protection pushes off the natural and logical consequences that the child should experience and that the child needs to learn to succeed in life.

Whether it is behavioral or grade issues, as parents, we should help the child to learn the consequences of their behavior and how to do better next time. It goes without saying that we should expect integrity, duty, excellence and friendliness from our children. The lesson for each parent is that there should <u>always</u> be age-appropriate consequences for the child's actions (good or bad). Robert A. Heinlein said, "Do not handicap your children by making their lives easy." **We should incrementally introduce our children to the stairways of life.**

Our third responsibility as a parent is to be an example to our children. Frequently parents complain that their children do not listen to them. In fact they listen all too well. As Ralph Waldo Emerson said, "Who you are speaks so loudly I can't hear what you're saying." That example starts with each of us accepting the natural and logical consequences of our own actions and explaining to our children, in age-appropriate terms, what we did correctly and the natural and logical consequences that followed, and what we did incorrectly and the natural and logical consequences that followed.

We don't have to be perfect (and we certainly won't be), but we should admit our errors and use them as both learning and teaching moments for both us and for our children. Our example continues with our self-challenge and pursuit of laudable life goals, our perseverance and hard work, our integrity, our focus on our duty, our drive for excellence, our self-discipline, our friendships and our career. Again, we must explain our example in age-appropriate terms to our children. An example in the integrity dimension is the quote from H. Jackson Brown Jr. who said, "Live so that when your children think of fairness and integrity, they think of you." **We must be a stair-climbing example to our children.**

The fourth most important responsibility of being a parent is to help our children find their goals in life. They must make their own path, but we need to help them experiment and understand the stairs that they need to climb. Brian Tracy said, "If you raise your children to feel that they can accomplish any goal or task they decide upon, you will have succeeded as a parent and you will have given your children the greatest of all blessings." **We should help our children find their own unique set of stairs to climb.**

Our fifth most important responsibility as a parent is to "push our children out of the nest." We need to incrementally grow their independence and include expectations that at some point they must prepare themselves and that they will make their own way in the world. **Over time we must learn to leave our children alone on their unique set of stairs.**

In summary, we take on our most requirements for stair-taking action when we become parents. Dr. James C. Dodson said, "Children are not casual guests in our home. They have been loaned to us temporarily for the purpose of loving them and instilling a foundation of values on which their future lives will be built." Our actions of selecting the right set of stairs for ourselves, climbing those stairs, and leading our children to become lifetime stair-climbers will be critical to our children's development.

1. **We must climb both the love and the discipline stairs for our children.** Robert A. Heinlein said, "Keep your children short on pocket money, but long on hugs."

2. **We should incrementally introduce our children to the stairways of life.** Lady Bird Johnson said, "Children are apt to live up to what you believe of them."

3. **We must be a stair-climbing example to our children.** James Arthur Baldwin said, "Children have never been very good at listening to their elders, but they have never failed to imitate them."

4. **We should help our children find their own unique sets of stairs to climb.** Brian Tracy said, "If you raise your children to feel that they can accomplish any goal or task they decide upon, you will have succeeded as a parent and you will have given your children the greatest of all blessings."

5. **Over time we must learn to leave our children alone on their unique set of stairs.** Henry C. Link said, "Psychologically I should say that a person becomes an adult at the point when he produces more than he consumes or earns more than he spends. This may be at the age of eighteen, twenty-five, or thirty-five."

Again, looking back now on the first two chapters, each of the five rules of stair climbing can now be stated in the dimension of raising your children. They are:

1. **Challenge:** We should challenge our children to age-appropriate laudable goals, hard work, integrity, duty, excellence, self-discipline and quality friendships. Alexander Chase said, "There are few successful adults who were not first successful children."

2. **Self-Assessment:** We should continuously self-assess our performance example in each of these dimensions and make continuous improvements. Dr Haim Ginott said, "Children are like wet cement. Whatever falls on them makes an impression."

3. **Preparation:** We should help prepare our children for real life. Robert Schuller said, "Spectacular achievement is always preceded by unspectacular preparation."

4. **Perseverance:** Raising children well is one of the most difficult challenges we will face. We will only be able to see real progress many years after the fact. We must persevere through the difficult times, and, in the process teach our children both our love and our perseverance. Thomas A. Edison said, "Our greatest weakness lies in giving up. The most certain way to succeed is always to try just one more time."

5. **Constancy:** We can never stop loving, teaching and mentoring our children. Garrison Keillor said, "Nothing you do for children is ever wasted. They seem not to notice us, hovering, averting our eyes, and they seldom offer thanks, but what we do for them is never wasted."

As with all else, when it comes to our children, we must take the stairs and teach them to take the stairs.

CONCLUSION

This book is really about our character, its development and its continuous improvement. Ralph Waldo Emerson said, "What lies behind us and what lies ahead of us are tiny matters compared to what lies within us." Only taking the stairs of life will develop our character. It's about laudable goals, hard work, integrity, duty, excellence, self-discipline and quality relationships. It's about taking the stairs in each of these dimensions.

None of us can predict the future, but we can learn to predict the consequences of our actions in terms of how they affect probable future outcomes, and in the process, significantly influence our future. The better that we become at this prediction process, the more thoughtful our planning and our actions will be. In summary, I have selected additional quotes on each of these dimensions.

1. **Challenge**: Douglas Lurtan said, "When you determine what you want, you have made the most important decision in your life. You have to know what you want in order to attain it." Albert Pine said, "What we do for ourselves dies with us. What we do for others and the world remains and is immortal."

2. **Perseverance**: Bruce Jenner said, "I learned that the only way you are going to get anywhere in life is to work hard at it. Whether you're a musician, a writer, an athlete, or a businessman, there is no getting around it. If you do, you'll win—if you don't, you won't."

3. **Integrity**: Andrew Carnegie said, "No amount of ability is of the slightest avail without honor."

4. **Duty**: Giuseppe Mazzini said, "Every mission constitutes a pledge of duty. Every man is bound to consecrate his every faculty to its fulfillment. He will derive his rule of action from the profound conviction of that duty."

5. **Excellence**: Confucius said, "There is one single thread binding my way together...the way of the Master consists in doing one's best...that is all."

6. **Self-Discipline**: Gautama Buddha said, "It is better to conquer yourself than to win a thousand battles. Then the

victory is yours. It cannot be taken from you, not by angels or by demons, heaven or hell."

7. **Friendships**: Ralph Waldo Emerson said, "The only reward of virtue is virtue; the only way to have a friend is to be one."

8. **Career:** C. Hoppe said, I hope that my achievements in life shall be these - that I will have fought for what was right and fair, that I will have risked for that which mattered, and that I will have given help to those who were in need that I will have left the earth a better place for what I've done and who I've been."

9. **Children:** John W. Whitehead said, "Children are the living messages we send to a time we will not see."

Repeating one of the quotes in Chapter 6, "Bum" Phillips said, "The only discipline that lasts is self-discipline." I would expand that quote to say that the only enforcement that lasts is self-enforcement. We must be our own enforcer with respect to our laudable goals, our work ethic, our integrity, our duty, our excellence, our self-discipline and the quality of our friendships. From a continued focus on each of these through the problems of life, we develop our courage. English writer C. S. Lewis said, "Courage is not simply one of the virtues, but the form of every virtue at the testing point."

With the final look-back now on the first two chapters, each of the five rules of stair climbing can be stated in all of the dimensions—laudable goals, work ethic, integrity, duty, excellence, self-discipline and quality relationships. They are:

1. **Challenge: We should challenge ourselves to laudable and challenging life goals, follow though with hard work, integrity, duty, excellence, self-discipline, and quality friendships and a satisfying career—in that**

order. Confucius said, "The will to win, the desire to succeed, the urge to reach your full potential... these are the keys that will unlock the door to personal excellence."

2. **Self-Assessment: We should continuously self-assess our performance in each of these dimensions and make continuous improvements.** James Allen said, "Men are anxious to improve their circumstances, but are unwilling to improve themselves; they therefore remain bound."

3. **Preparation: We should prepare for the difficult times in each of these dimensions by practice at every opportunity.** Ben Franklin said, "By failing to prepare, you are preparing to fail."

4. **Perseverance: We should persevere through the difficult times and never give up in any one of these dimensions—our life goals, hard work, integrity, duty, excellence, self-discipline, quality friendships and our career goals.** Maya Angelou said, "We will sometimes have defeats in life but you can have defeats without being defeated, you can fail without being a failure. Winners see failure and defeats as merely part of the process to get to win."

5. **Constancy: We can never stop our journey on the stairs.** An unknown author said, "Success is not a destination, it's the journey."

Mahatma Gandhi said, "Keep my words positive, because my words become behaviors. Keep my behaviors positive, because my behaviors become habits. Keep my habit positive, because my habits become my values. Keep my values positive, because they become my destiny."

In conclusion, **each of us must challenge ourselves to laudable life goals, persevere through hard work and take the stairs when it comes to integrity, duty, excellence, self-discipline, quality friendships, our career and raising our children.** I look forward to seeing each of you on the stairs.

APPENDIX OF
QUOTATIONS

The Internet has become an outstanding source for initial research, for finding relevant quotations and then verifying them from other sources. The following major sources were invaluable for that research:

1. Google (http://www.google.com).

2. Wikipedia (http://en.wikipedia.org/wiki/Main_Page).

3. The Quotations Page (http://www.quotationspage.com).

4. Quotations Book (http://www.quotationsbook.com).

5. Wisdom Quotes (http://www.wisdomquotes.com).

6. Think Exist (http://en.thinkexist.com).

7. Leadership Now (http://www.leadershipnow.com).

8. Brainy Quote (http://www.brainyquote.com).

9. Quote Garden (http://www.quotegarden.com).

Beginning

1. "Success is dependent upon effort." Sophocles—Greek tragic dramatist (496 BC - 406 BC).

Chapter 1—Challenge and Self-Assessment

1. "The journey of a thousand miles begins with a single step." Lau-Tzu—Chinese philosopher (604 BC - 531 BC).

2. "You got to be careful if you don't know where you're going, because you might not get there." Yogi Berra—US baseball player, coach, & manager (1925 -).

3. "Insanity is doing the same thing over and over and expecting different results." Ben Franklin—US author, diplomat, inventor, physicist, politician, & printer (1706 - 1790).

4. "In the long run, you hit only what you aim at: Therefore aim high." Henry David Thoreau—US Transcendentalist author (1817 - 1862).

5. "I'm a great believer in luck, and I find the harder I work the more I have of it." Thomas Jefferson—Third US President (1743 - 1826).

6. "Become addicted to constant and never-ending self-improvement." Anthony J. D'Angelo—US inspirational writer (1972 -).

7. "Ask not what your country can do for you - ask what you can do for your country." John F. Kennedy—35th US President (1917 – 1963).

8. "People thought it was asinine for me to change my swing after I won the Masters by 12 shots. ... Why would you want to change that? Well, I thought I could become better." Tiger Woods—US professional golfer (1975 -).

9. "Argue for your limitations and, sure enough they're yours." Richard Bach, Jonathan Livingston Seagull—US inspirational writer (1936 -).

10. "The price of success is hard work, dedication to the job at hand, and the determination that whether we win or lose, we have applied the best of ourselves to the task at hand." Vince Lombardi—US professional (and West Point) football coach (1913 - 1970).

Chapter 2—Preparation, Perseverance and Constancy

1. "Be Prepared." Lord Robert Baden-Powell—English founder of the Boy Scouts (1857 - 1941).

2. "Unless a man has trained himself for his chance, the chance will only make him look ridiculous. A great occasion is worth to man exactly what his preparation enables him to make of it." J. B. Matthews—US author and activist (1894 – 1966).

3. "Before everything else, getting ready is the secret to success." Henry Ford—US automobile industrialist (1863 - 1947).

4. "It is not the critic who counts, not the man who points out how the strong man stumbled, or where the doer of deeds could have done better. The credit belongs to the man who is actually in the arena, whose face is marred by dust and sweat and blood, who strives valiantly, who errs and comes short again and again, who knows the great enthusiasms, the great devotions, and spends himself in a worthy cause, who at best knows achievement and who at the worst if he fails at least fails while daring greatly so that his place shall never be with those cold and timid souls who know neither victory nor defeat." Theodore Roosevelt—26th US President (1858 - 1919).

5. "Don't let what you cannot do interfere with what you can do." John Wooden—US basketball coach (1910 -).

6. "Experience is what you get when you don't get what you want." Dan Stanford—US inspirational writer.

7. "Excellence is not something attained & put in a trophy case. It is not sought after, achieved, and, thereafter, a steady state. It is a momentary phenomenon, a rare conjunction of body, mind and spirit at one's peak. Should I come to that peak, I cannot stay there. Like Sisyphus, I must start each day at the bottom & work back up to the top. And then beyond that peak to another and yet another." Dr. George Sheehan—US runner, author and philosopher (1918 – 1993).

8. "Talent is cheaper than table salt. What separates the talented individual from the successful one is a lot of hard work." Stephen King—US horror novelist & screenwriter (1947 -).

9. "Goals are not only absolutely necessary to motivate us. They are essential to really keep us alive." Dr. Robert H. Schuller—US minister (1926 -).

10. "Let us strive to improve ourselves, for we cannot remain stationary; one either progresses or retrogrades." Marie Anne de Vichy-Chamrond, marquise du Deffand—French patron of the arts (1697 -1780).

11. "It's not the will to win, but the will to prepare to win that makes the difference." Paul William "Bear" Bryant—US college football coach (1913 – 1983).

12. "If you run into a wall, don't turn around and give up. Figure out how to climb it, go through it, or work your way around it." Michael Jordan—US professional basketball player (1963 -).

13. "All great masters are chiefly distinguished by the power of adding a second, a third, and perhaps a fourth step in a continuous line. Many a man has taken the first step. With every additional step you enhance immensely the value of your first." Ralph Waldo Emerson—US essayist & poet (1803 - 1882).

14. "But choose wisely, for while the true Grail will bring you life, the false Grail will take it from you." The Grail Knight, Indiana Jones and the Last Crusade (1989).

Chapter 3—Integrity

1. "The supreme quality for leadership is unquestionably integrity. Without it, no real success is possible, no matter whether it is on a section gang, a football field, in an army, or in an office." Dwight D. Eisenhower—US General, 34th US President and 1915 West Point graduate (1890 -1969).

2. "If you have integrity, nothing else matters. If you don't have integrity, nothing else matters."   Alan K. Simpson—US Senator (1931 -).

3. "Truth has no special time of its own. Its hour is now— always".   Albert Schweitzer—French philosopher & physician (1875 - 1965).

4. "A promise made is a debt unpaid." Robert W. Service— Canadian poet (1874 - 1958).

5. "Real integrity is doing the right thing, knowing that nobody's going to know whether you did it or not." Oprah Winfrey, in Good Housekeeping—US television talk show hostess and actress (1954 -).

6. "You can discover more about a person in an hour of play than in a year of conversation." Plato—Greek author & philosopher (427 BC - 347 BC).

7. "Rather fall with honor than succeed by fraud". Sophocles—Greek tragic dramatist (496 BC - 406 BC).

8. "The only thing necessary for the triumph of evil is for good men to do nothing." Edmond Burke—Irish orator, philosopher, & politician (1729 - 1797).

9. "If you would lift me up you must be on higher ground." Ralph Waldo Emerson—US essayist & poet (1803 - 1882).

10. "Truth is the only safe ground to stand on." Elizabeth Cady Stanton—US suffragette (1815-1902).

11. "It is not the oath that makes us believe the man, but the man the oath." Aeschylus—Greek playwright (525 BC – 456 BC).

12. "So act that your principle of action might safely be made a law for the whole world." Immanuel Kant—German philosopher (1724 - 1804).

13. "Whenever you do a thing, act as if all the world were watching." Thomas Jefferson—Third US President (1743 - 1826).

14. "To know what is right and not do it is the worst cowardice." Confucius—Chinese philosopher & reformer (551 BC - 479 BC).

15. "Relativity applies to physics, not ethics." Albert Einstein—US (German born) theoretical physicist (1879 – 1955).

16. "He who stops being better stops being good." Oliver Cromwell—English military leader (1599 – 1658).

17. "The time is always right to do what is right." Martin Luther King Jr.—US minister and civil rights leader (1928 – 1968).

18. "Moral courage is the most valuable and usually the most absent characteristic in men." George S. Patton—US General and 1909 West Point graduate (1885 - 1945).

19. "The question is not whether we will die, but how we will live." Joan Borysenko—US psychologist and author.

20. "Regard your good name as the richest jewel you can possibly be possessed of - for credit is like fire; when once you have kindled it you may easily preserve it, but if you once extinguish it, you will find it an arduous task to rekindle it again. The way to gain a good reputation is to endeavor to be what you desire to appear." Socrates—Greek philosopher (469 BC - 399 BC).

Chapter 4—Duty

1. "Duty then is the sublimest (sic) word in the English language. You should do your duty in all things. You can never do more. You should never wish to do less." Robert E. Lee—US Confederate General and 1829 West Point graduate (1807 - 1870).

2. "American Express, membership has its privileges. ®" American Express Company Registered Trade Mark.

3. "Do your duty and a little more and the future will take care of itself." Andrew Carnegie—US businessman and philanthropist (1835 - 1919).

4. "Never mind your happiness; Do your duty." Peter Drucker—US (Austrian born) management and leadership author (1909 – 2005).

5. "Conscientious people are apt to see their duty in that which is the most painful course." George Eliot (pseudonym for Mary Anne Evans)—English novelist (1819 - 1880).

6. "Do the duty which lies nearest to you, the second duty will then become clearer." Thomas Carlyle—Scottish essayist (1795 – 1881).

7. "Duty is not collective; it is personal." Calvin Coolidge—30th US President (1872-1933).

8. "The strength of the team is each individual member…the strength of each member is the team." Phil Jackson—Basketball Coach (1945-).

9. "We are all in the same boat in a stormy sea, and we owe each other a terrible loyalty." G. K. (Gilbert Keith) Chesterton—Journalist, Novelist (1874-1936).

10. "Activate yourself to duty by remembering your position, who you are, and what you have obliged yourself to be." Thomas Kempis—German mystic & religious author (1380 - 1471).

11. "You cannot hope to build a better world without improving the individuals. To that end each of us must work for his own improvement and at the same time share a general responsibility for all humanity, our particular duty being to aid those to whom we think we can be most useful." French scientist Marie Curie—French (Polish-born) chemist & physicist (1867 - 1934).

12. "Do something every day that you don't want to do; this is the golden rule for acquiring the habit of doing your duty without pain." Mark Twain (pseudonym for Samuel Longhorn Clemens)—US humorist and novelist (1835 - 1910).

13. "My duty is clear and at all costs will be done." John Burns—English activist (1858 – 1943).

14. "We never fail when we try to do our duty; we always fail when we neglect to do it." Lord Robert Baden-Powell—English founder of the Boy Scouts (1857 - 1941).

15. "No snowflake in an avalanche ever feels responsible." Voltaire (pseudonym for François-Marie Arouet)—French writer and philosopher (1694 – 1778).

Chapter 5—Excellence

1. "If I had to build an outhouse, then I would build the best damn outhouse that the US Army has ever seen." John J. (Black Jack) Pershing—US General and 1886 West Point graduate (1860 – 1948).

2. "When you do the common things in life in an uncommon way, you will command the attention of the world." George Washington Carver—US inventor and professor (1864 – 1943).

3. "If you are going to achieve excellence in big things, you develop the habit in little matters. Excellence is not an exception, it is a prevailing attitude." Colin Powell—US General and Secretary of State (1937 -).

4. "We are what we repeatedly do. Excellence, then, is not an act but a habit."   Aristotle—Greek critic, philosopher, physicist, & zoologist (384 BC - 322 BC).

5. "Excellence means when a man or woman asks of himself more than others do."   José Ortega Y Gassett—Spanish philosopher (1883 – 1955).

6. "A thought which does not result in an action is nothing much, and an action which does not proceed from a thought is nothing at all."   Georges Bernanos—French author and WWI soldier (1888 – 1848).

7. "If you cannot do great things, do small things in a great way."   Napoleon Hill—US author (1883 – 1970).

8. "There is always a best way of doing everything."   Ralph Waldo Emerson—US essayist & poet (1803 - 1882).

9. "The quality of a person's life is in direct proportion to their commitment to excellence, regardless of their chosen field of endeavor."   Vince Lombardi—US professional and West Point football coach (1913 – 1970).

10. "It takes a long time to bring excellence to maturity."   Publilius Syrus—ancient Roman writer (~100 BC).

11. "If you want to achieve excellence, you can get there today. As of this second, quit doing less-than-excellent work."   Thomas J. Watson—US businessman and founder of IBM (1874 – 1956).

12. "Remember that the most difficult tasks are consummated, not by a single explosive burst of energy or effort, but by the constant daily application of the best you have within you."   Og Mandino—US inspirational writer (1923 – 1996).

13. "I do the very best I know how - the very best I can; and I mean to keep on doing so until the end." Abraham Lincoln—16th US President (1809 – 1865).

14. "Every job is a self-portrait of the person who did it. Autograph your work with excellence." Jessica Guidobono—Canadian author.

Chapter 6—Self Discipline

1. "With self-discipline most anything is possible." Theodore Roosevelt—26th US President (1858 - 1919).

2. "The only discipline that lasts is self-discipline." Oail Andrew "Bum" Phillips—NFL football coach (1923 -).

3. "Pain is temporary. Quitting lasts forever." Lance Armstrong—US professional cyclist and cancer survivor (1971 -).

4. "Self-discipline is an act of cultivation. It requires you to connect today's actions to tomorrow's results. There's a season for sowing, a season for reaping. Self-discipline helps you know which is which." Gary Ryan Blair—US motivational speaker.

5. "…kill two birds with one stone…" old English idiom meaning to do two things at the same time using the effort needed to do only one.

6. "The road to Hell is paved with good intentions." Sixteenth century proverb.

7. "First we make our habits: then our habits make us." Charles C. Noble—US General and CEO (1850 – 2003).

8. "If I knew I was going to live this long, I'd have taken better care of myself." Mickey Mantle—US baseball player (1931 – 1995).

9. "Just like Superman, each of us has our potential 'kryptonite'." Michael Drabant—US Attorney and our son (1982 -).

10. "We all have dreams. But in order to make dreams come into reality, it takes an awful lot of determination, dedication, self-discipline, and effort." Jesse Owens—US Olympic athlete (1913 – 1980).

11. "Efficiency is doing things right; effectiveness is doing the right things." Peter F. Drucker—US management author (1909 – 2005).

12. "Wisdom is knowing what to do next; virtue is doing it." David Starr Jordan—US ichthyologist and Stanford University President (1851 – 1931).

13. "It is not the mountain we conquer but ourselves." Sir Edmund Hillary—New Zealand mountaineer, explorer and conqueror of Mt. Everest (1919 - 2008).

14. "One can have no smaller or greater mastery than mastery of oneself." Leonardo da Vinci—painter, architect, engineer, mathematician and philosopher (1452 – 1519).

15. "By constant self-discipline and self-control you can develop greatness of character." Grenville Kleiser—US author (1868 - 1935).

16. "We should every night call ourselves to an account; what infirmity have I mastered today? What passions opposed? What temptation resisted? What virtue acquired? Our vices will abort of themselves if they be brought every day to the shrift." Lucius Annaeus Seneca—Roman playwright and philosopher (3 BC – 35 A.D).

17. "In reading the lives of great men, I found that the first victory they won was over themselves...self-discipline with all of them came first." Harry S. Truman—33rd US President (1884 – 1972).

18. "What you think is the top, is only a step." Lucius Annaeus Seneca—Roman playwright and philosopher (3 BC – 35 A.D).

19. "The first and best victory is to conquer self." Plato—Greek author & philosopher (427 BC - 347 BC).

Chapter 7—Friendship

1. "No man is an island, entire of itself...any man's death diminishes me, because I am involved in mankind; and therefore never send to know for whom the bell tolls; it tolls for thee." John Donne—English poet and writer (1572 – 1631).

2. "The only way to have a friend is to be one." Ralph Waldo Emerson—US essayist & poet (1803 - 1882).

3. "Be courteous to all, but intimate with few, and let those few be well tried before you give them your confidence. True friendship is a plant of slow growth, and must undergo and withstand the shocks of adversity before it is entitled to the appellation." George Washington—First US President (1732 -1799).

4. "You don't make friends, you earn them." Author unknown.

5. "You can easily judge the character of a man by how he treats those who can do nothing for him." James D. Miles—US author.

6. "When you're part of a team, you stand up for your teammates. Your loyalty is to them. You protect them through good and bad, because they'd do the same for you." Yogi Berra—US baseball player, coach, & manager (1925 -).

7. "...refrigerator friends—those people with whom we feel enough comfort to help ourselves to the food in their refrigerators." Dr. Will Miller—US motivational speaker.

8. "Have no friends not equal to yourself." Confucius, The Analects—Chinese philosopher & reformer (551 BC - 479 BC).

9. "When the character of a man is not clear to you, look at his friends." Ancient Japanese proverb.

10. "Misfortune shows those who are not really friends." Aristotle—Greek critic, philosopher, physicist, & zoologist (384 BC - 322 BC).

11. "If a man does not make new acquaintance as he advances through life, he will soon find himself left alone. A man, Sir, should keep his friendships in constant repair." Samuel Johnson—British lexicographer (1709 – 1784).

12. "Sometimes it's a little better to travel than to arrive." Robert M. Pirsig, <u>Zen and the Art of Motorcycle Maintenance</u>—US author (1928 -).

13. "Friendship without self interest is one of the rare and beautiful things in life." James Francis Byrnes—US politician (1879 – 1972).

14. "Friendship is held to be the severest test of character. It is easy, we think, to be loyal to a family and clan, whose blood is in your own veins. Love between a man and a woman is founded on the mating instinct and is not free from desire and self-seeking. But to have a friend and to be true under any and all trials is the mark of a man!" Charles Alexander Eastman—Native American author and physician (1858 – 1939).

15. "Truly great friends are hard to find, difficult to leave, and impossible to forget." G. Randolf—US author.

16. "Whoever says Friendship is easy has obviously never had a true friend!" Bronwyn Polson—Australian author.

17. "My best friend is the one who brings out the best in me." Henry Ford—US automobile industrialist (1863 – 1947).

18. "Always be a little kinder than necessary." James M Barrie— Scottish author and playwright (1860 – 1937).

19. "Forgive many things in others; nothing in yourself." Decimus Magnus Ausonius—Roman poet (310 – 395).

20. "The better part of one's life consists of his friendships." Abraham Lincoln—16th US President (1809 – 1865).

21. "True friendship consists not in the multitude of friends, but in their worth and value." Ben Johnson—English playwright (1572 – 1637).

22. "The making of friends, who are real friends, is the best token we have of a man's success in life." Edward Everett Hale—US author (1822 – 1909).

Chapter 8—Career

1. "My mother drew a distinction between achievement and success. She said that 'achievement is the knowledge that you have studied and worked hard and done the best that is in you. Success is being praised by others, and that's nice, too, but not as important or satisfying. Always aim for achievement and forget about success.'" Helen Hayes—US actress (1900 – 1993).

2. "TANSTAAFL. There ain't (sic) no such thing as a free lunch." Robert A. Heinlein, The Moon Is a Harsh Mistress—US science fiction writer and 1929 USNA (Annapolis) graduate (1907 – 1988).

3. "I Don't Do Windows" Country and western song by Willie Nelson and Hank Cochran.

4. "The best augury of a man's success in his profession is that he thinks it the finest in the world." George Eliot (pseudonym for Mary Anne Evans)—English novelist (1819 - 1880).

5. "Be true to your work, your word, and your friend." Henry David Thoreau—US author (1817 – 1872).

6. "The difference between a job and a career is the difference between forty and sixty hours a week." Robert Frost—US poet (1874 – 1963).

7. "The life-fate of the modern individual depends not only upon the family into which he was born or which he enters by marriage, but increasingly upon the corporation in which he spends the most alert hours of his best years." C. Wright Mills—US sociologist (1916 – 1962).

8. "No man ever reached to excellence in any one art or profession without having passed through the slow and painful process of study and preparation." Horace—Ancient Roman poet (65 BC – 8 BC).

9. "Nothing of great value in life comes easily." Dr. Norman Vincent Peale—US minister and author (1898 – 1993).

10. "The individual who wants to reach the top in business must appreciate the might and force of habit. He must be quick to break those habits that can break him—and hasten to adopt those practices that will become the habits that help him achieve the success he desires." J. Paul Getty—US oil industrialist (1892 – 1976).

11. "To be prepared is half the victory." Miguel de Cervantes—Spanish novelist (1547 – 1616).

12. "History has demonstrated that the most notable winners usually encountered heartbreaking obstacles before they triumphed. They won because they refused to become discouraged by their defeats." B. C. (Bertie Charles) Forbes—US founder of Forbes magazine (1880 – 1954).

13. "Success is a journey, not a destination. The doing is often more important than the outcome." Arthur Ashe—US professional tennis player (1943 – 1993).

Chapter 9-Children

1. "What the vast majority of American children need is to stop being pampered, stop being indulged, stop being chauffeured, and stop being catered to. In the final analysis it is not what you do for your children but what you have taught them to do for themselves that will make them successful human beings." Ann Landers (Esther "Eppie" Pauline Friedman Lederer)—US advice columnist (1918 – 2002).

2. "Even though your kids will consistently do the exact opposite of what you're telling them to do, you have to keep loving them just as much." Bill Cosby—US actor, writer and comedian (1937 -).

3. "Do not handicap your children by making their lives easy." Robert A. Heinlein—US science fiction writer and 1929 USNA (Annapolis) graduate (1907 – 1988).

4. "Who you are speaks so loudly I can't hear what you're saying." Ralph Waldo Emerson—US essayist & poet (1803 - 1882).

5. "Live so that when your children think of fairness and integrity, they think of you." H. Jackson Brown Jr.—US inspirational author.

6. "If you raise your children to feel that they can accomplish any goal or task they decide upon, you will have succeeded as a parent and you will have given your children the greatest of all blessings." Brian Tracy—Canadian inspirational writer and speaker (1944 -).

7. "Children are not casual guests in our home. They have been loaned to us temporarily for the purpose of loving them and instilling a foundation of values on which their future lives will be built." Dr. James C. Dobson—US minister (1936 -).

8. "Keep your children short on pocket money and long on hugs." Robert A Heinlein—US science fiction writer and 1929 USNA (Annapolis) graduate (1907 – 1988).

9. "Children are apt to live up to what you believe of them." Lady Bird Johnson—US first lady and wife of 36th US President Lyndon Johnson (1912 -).

10. "Children have never been very good at listening to their elders, but they have never failed to imitate them." James Arthur Baldwin—US essayist, playwright and novelist (1924-1987).

11. "If you raise your children to feel that they can accomplish any goal or task they decide upon, you will have succeeded as a parent and you will have given your children the greatest of all blessings." Brian Tracy—Canadian inspirational writer and speaker (1944 -).

12. "Psychologically I should say that a person becomes an adult at the point when he produces more than he consumes or earns more than he spends. This may be at the age of eighteen, twenty-five, or thirty-five." Henry C. Link—US author.

13. "There are few successful adults who were not first successful children." Alexander Chase—US author.

14. "Children are like wet cement. Whatever falls on them makes an impression." Dr Haim Ginott—US child psychologist and author (1922-1973).

15. "Spectacular achievement is always preceded by unspectacular preparation." Dr. Robert H. Schuller—US minister (1926 -).

16. "Our greatest weakness lies in giving up. The most certain way to succeed is always to try just one more time." Thomas A. Edison—US inventor (1847 – 1931).

17. "Nothing you do for children is ever wasted. They seem not to notice us, hovering, averting our eyes, and they seldom offer thanks, but what we do for them is never wasted." Garrison Keillor—US author and humorist (1942 -).

Conclusion

1. "What lies behind us and what lies ahead of us are tiny matters compared to what lies within us." Ralph Waldo Emerson—US essayist & poet (1803 - 1882).

2. "When you determine what you want, you have made the most important decision in your life. You have to know what you want in order to attain it." Douglas Lurtan—US author.

3. "What we do for ourselves dies with us. What we do for others and the world remains and is immortal." Albert Pine—English author (1808 - 1851).

4. "I learned that the only way you are going to get anywhere in life is to work hard at it. Whether you're a musician, a writer, an athlete, or a businessman, there is no getting around it. If you do, you'll win—if you don't, you won't." Bruce Jenner—US Olympic athlete (1949 -).

5. "No amount of ability is of the slightest avail without honor." Andrew Carnegie—US businessman and philanthropist (1835 – 1919).

6. "Every mission constitutes a pledge of duty. Every man is bound to consecrate his every faculty to its fulfillment. He will derive his rule of action from the profound conviction of that duty." Giuseppe Mazzini—Italian patriot, politician and philosopher (1805 – 1872).

7. "The Master said, 'Ts'an! There is one single thread binding my way together.' Tseng Tzu assented. After the Master had gone out, the disciples asked, 'What did he mean?' Tseng Tzu said, 'The way of the Master consists in doing one's best and in using oneself as a measure to gauge others. That is all.'" Confucius, The Analects—Chinese philosopher & reformer (551 BC - 479 BC).

8. "It is better to conquer yourself than to win a thousand battles. Then the victory is yours. It cannot be taken from you, not by angels or by demons, heaven or hell." Gautama Buddha (Siddhartha Gautama)—founder of Buddhism (~500 BC - ~420 BC).

9. "The only reward of virtue is virtue; the only way to have a friend is to be one." Ralph Waldo Emerson—US essayist & poet (1803 - 1882).

10. "I hope that my achievements in life shall be these - that I will have fought for what was right and fair, that I will have risked for that which mattered, and that I will have given help to those who were in need that I will have left the earth a better place for what I've done and who I've been." C. Hoppe—US author.

11. "Children are the living messages we send to a time we will not see." John W. Whitehead—US attorney and author (1946 -).

12. "Courage is not simply one of the virtues, but the form of every virtue at the testing point." C. S. (Clive Staples) Lewis—Irish author (1898 – 1963).

13. "The will to win, the desire to succeed, the urge to reach your full potential... these are the keys that will unlock the door to personal excellence." Confucius—Chinese philosopher & reformer (551 BC - 479 BC).

14. "Men are anxious to improve their circumstances, but are unwilling to improve themselves; they therefore remain bound." James Allen—English inspirational writer (1864 – 1912).

15. "By failing to prepare, you are preparing to fail." Ben Franklin—US author, diplomat, inventor, physicist, politician, & printer (1706 - 1790).

16. "We will sometimes have defeats in life but you can have defeats without being defeated, you can fail without being a failure. Winners see failure and defeats as merely part of the process to get to win." Dr. Maya Angelou—US poet and author (1928 -).

17. "Success is not a destination, it's the journey." Author unknown.

18. "Keep my words positive, because my words become behaviors. Keep my behaviors positive, because my behaviors become habits. Keep my habit positive, because my habits become my values. Keep my values positive, because they become my destiny." Mahatma Gandhi—Indian political and spiritual leader (1869 – 1948).

APPENDIX OF PHOTOS

All photographs were taken at USAFA by the author.

1. Cover page—Vandenberg Hall northeast stairwell at sunrise.

2. Dedication—Stairs to the honor court north of Harman Hall and the Chapel.

3. Acknowledgements—Stairs to the Barry Goldwater Visitor Center.

4. Table of Contents—Stairs on the north side of Falcon Stadium.

5. Beginning—Vandenberg Hall northeast stairwell at the bottom of the stairs.

6. Chapter 1—Ten meter diving tower over the Olympic pool inside the Cadet Gymnasium.

7. Chapter 2—Stairs from Pine Valley to the Community Center.

8. Chapter 3—Stairs at the main entrance to the Cadet Chapel.

9. Chapter 4—Cadet Obstacle Course in Jacks Valley.

10. Chapter 5—Stairs from the Cadet Gymnasium to Vandenberg Hall.

11. Chapter 6—Cadet Obstacle Course in Jacks Valley.

12. Chapter 7—Stairwell in Fairchild Hall.

13. Chapter 8—Looking up the circular stairwell in the McDermott Library in Fairchild Hall.

14. Chapter 9—Stairs in Arnold Hall leading to the theater balcony.

15. Conclusion and back cover—Looking down the circular stairwell in the McDermott Library in Fairchild Hall.

16. Appendix of Quotations—Stairs between Mitchell and Sijan Halls to the Terrazzo.

Made in the USA